THE APPOINTED EARTH

THE APPOINTED EARTH

Literary Reflections on the Creation

NORMAN CHANEY

First Edition
September 2017

Book cover design by Norman and Freda Chaney

ISBN-13: 9781533521965
ISBN-10: 1533521964

To Freda—my spiritual accomplice

CONTENTS

PHOTOGRAPHS

ACKNOWLEDGMENTS

I AM GRATEFUL to students, colleagues, and conference participants who over years have listened to me muse over subjects expressed in this book. Most of all I am grateful to my wife, Freda, who has taken photographs and kept notes throughout our many travels in conjunction with our love of literature and the world of nature. All photographs are hers, with the exception of the Hurt Hawk photograph in Chapter 3. It appears by generous permission of Angela Demetriou–McClain. The Notes and Bibliography contained in this book relate to the writers I have considered. I am grateful to numerous other writers I have had no cause to name, who have inspired me in their singing of hallelujahs to the glories of the creation.

INTRODUCTION

THOMAS DE QUINCEY in an essay on Alexander Pope drew the distinction between the literature of knowledge and the literature of power. The literature of knowledge conveys information and makes its appeal to the reason. The literature of power may also convey information, but its appeal is to the sympathies, the emotions, and the imagination as well as to reason.[1]

In this book, I do not deny that the Holy Bible is a literature of knowledge, but I emphasize it as a literature of power. At least part of inspiration in the writing of the Bible was the quickening of the imaginations of gifted writers, to whom it was given to see visions and to dream dreams. They were writers who spoke as they were moved about a divine creation of all things, and whose words, through all the accidents and handicaps of literary transmission, have spoken and continue to speak to persons who listen.

A person who listened was Caedmon (died c. AD 680), the earliest recorded poet of sacred song in English literary tradition. In his *Ecclesiastical History of the English People* (AD 731), the Venerable Bede tells briefly the story of Caedmon's life. Caedmon was an illiterate keeper of livestock at the monastery of Whitby, who was sometimes privy to biblical recitations of monks within the abbey. One night when he was on duty in the stable, he fell asleep and had a dream. In the dream, a man appeared and commanded Caedmon to sing. He protested that he could not sing. "You shall sing to me, "The man insisted. "But what should I sing about"? Caedmon asked. And the man said, "Sing about the Creation of all things." And immediately, says Bede, Caedmon "began to sing verses in praise of God the Creator":

> Praise we the Fashioner now of Heaven's fabric,
> The majesty of his might and his mind's wisdom,
> Work of the world-warden, worker of all wonders,
> How he the Lord of Glory everlasting,
> Wrought first for the race of men Heaven as a rooftree,
> Then made he Middle Earth to be their mansion.[2]

Modern science and technology have peered ever more deeply into the wonders of our "own cosmic habitat."[3] In our thinking and speaking about these wonders, biblical language is hardly passé. When in December 1968 the Apollo astronauts made their journey to orbit the moon, they looked out to see the earth spinning against the frozen darkness of space like a blue and white mottled marble, they found words to describe what they saw and felt in language of the Bible. They took turns reading from Genesis 1: 1–10, from the King James Version.

Bill Anders
In the beginning God created the heaven and the earth.
And the earth was without form, and void; and darkness was
upon the face of the deep.
And the Spirit of God moved upon the face of the waters. And God said, Let
there be light: and there was light.
And God saw the light, that it was good: and God divided the light from the darkness.
Jim Lovell
And God called the light Day, and the darkness he called Night. And the evening
and the morning were the first day.

And God said, Let there be a firmament in the midst of the waters, and let it divide the waters from the waters. And God made the firmament, and divided the waters which were under the firmament from the waters which were above the firmament: and it was so. And God called the firmament Heaven. And the evening and the morning were the second day.*

Frank Borman

And God said, Let the waters under the heaven be gathered together unto one place, and let the dry land appear: and it was so. And God called the dry land Earth; and the gathering together of the waters called he Seas: and God saw that it was good.

I speak in this book of writers who have helped me over years to sustain confidence in and wonder of a creation that is "appointed"[4] by and permeated with *something* not our own. That *something* may be called by various names, such as: *Creator, God, "I Am," Being, Presence, Essence, Power, Principle, Numen, Spirit, Life,* or *Intelligence.* My own preferred name for the *something* is *Wisdom,* which I borrow from Proverbs 8:1.

Walt Whitman offered advice about how to open ourselves to the *something* when he wrote:

> You must not know too much, or be too precise or scientific about birds and trees and flowers and watercraft; a certain free margin, and even vagueness—perhaps ignorance, credulity—helps your enjoyment of these things.[5]

Henry David Thoreau offered advice similar to Whitman's when in response to a friend's question about his religious convictions, Thoreau answered:

Let God alone if need be. Methinks, if I loved him more, I should keep him,—I should keep myself rather,—at a more respectful distance. It is not when I am going to meet him, but when I am just turning away and leaving him alone, that I discover that God is. I say, God. I am not sure that that is the name. You will know whom I mean.[6]

My choice of writers to consider in this book is eclectic, but not arbitrary. They offer, individually and collectively, as the biblical writers did, reflections on the creation that evoke wonder of a Wisdom that fills the universe. It might be thought because I consider various writers' reflections on the world of nature that I do not have my own to express. Mine is embodied in "God's in the Dirt," and "A Testimonial Epilogue."

Biblical quotations throughout this book are taken from a leather-bound, duodecimo-size Bible—The Authorized King James Version—that my parents gave me on my sixteenth birthday: The Holy Bible, ed. Rev. C. I. Scofield, D.D. (New York: Oxford University Press, 1945). The rhetorical eloquence of the King James Version (1611) has not been exceeded in subsequent English translations.

I do not intend this book as a work of innovative scholarship, although studious investigation has been part of its making. Emerson wrote, "First we eat, then we beget; first we read, then we write."[7] I have let what others have said shine on my reading of these writers. I trust I have duly acknowledged in text, and Notes, and Bibliography my indebtedness to critics, historians, philosophers, and theologians who have informed my readings. The readings themselves are mine. Their personal tone is intended.

NOTES

1. Thomas De Quincey, *Leaders in Literature with Notice of Traditional Errors Affecting Them* (Edinburgh: Adam and Charles Black, 1887), 10.
2. Bede, *trans. Leo Sherley-Price, rev. R. E. Latham, Ecclesiastical History of the English People* (New York: Penguin Books, 1990), 248-49.
3. Martin Rees, *Our Cosmic Habitat* (Princeton: Princeton University Press, 2001), xvii.
4. Prov. 8:29. As mentioned in the Introduction, biblical citations throughout this book are from the Authorized King James Version of the Bible; cited by book and verse numbers.
5. Walt Whitman, *Specimen Days and Collect* (New York: Dove Publications, Inc., 1995), 183.
6. Henry David Thoreau, *Henry David Thoreau: Letters to a Spiritual Seeker* (New York: W. W. Norton and Company, 2004), 53.
7. Ralph Waldo Emerson, *The Journals and Notebooks of Ralph Waldo Emerson*, eds. William H. Gilman and J. E. Parson (Cambridge: Harvard University Press, 1970), Vol. VIII, 320.

1

RICHARD JEFFERIES:
THE NATURE WRITER AS INNOCENT ADAM

*There are innocent men who worship God after the
tradition of their fathers,
but their sense of duty has not yet extended to the use
of all their faculties.*

—RALPH WALDO EMERSON, *NATURE*

WHEN THE LORD created the heavens and "appointed the foundations of the earth"[1] his creation included an earthly garden that reflected Paradise. The Lord enjoyed walking in the garden in the cool of the evening, sometimes conversing with the two humans he had placed there as its original inhabitants. It was a sad day when the Lord discovered that the two humans had broken his rule not to eat the fruit of a particular tree. He did not have to give a reason for this rule. After all, it was his garden, his tree, and his rule. It was even a sadder day when an angel of the Lord escorted the two humans out of the garden for having broken the Lord's rule. "Som natural tears they drop'd," Milton tells us at the end of *Paradise Lost*, but they

> wip'd them soon;
> The world was all before them, where to choose
> Thir place of rest, and Providence thir quide;
> They hand in hand with wandring steps and slow,
> Through Eden took thir solitary way.[2]

Our original parents lost the garden, but human life, as the biblical story continues, involves a circuitous journey. In sending Adam and Eve forth from the garden, the Lord endowed them with a curiosity that made them seekers of a lost happiness in a world of pain, sickness, and death. At the end of the circuitous journey, the writer of Revelation foretells, children of Adam and Eve, the blistering experiences of history behind them, will journey back to the Heavenly Paradise from whence they originally derived. In that Heavenly Paradise, "Every creature which is in heaven and on the earth, and under the earth, and such as are in the sea," will join in singing to their Creator "Blessing and honor and glory and power . . . for ever and ever."[3]

In offering this summary version of the biblical story of creation, I am reminded of T. S. Eliot's words:

That was a way of putting it—not very satisfactory:
A periphrastic study in a worn-out poetical fashion,
Leaving one still with the intolerable wrestle
With words and meanings.[4]

It is widely held in our time that the story of creation encapsulated in the Bible is spent. The philosopher Charles Taylor reflects that with developments in science over the last half millennium the biblical story of a Creator who initiates and oversees all temporal and physical reality is "hard to understand, or even imagine."[5] The biblical writers did not know, as we know today, that we live on a planet circling a medium-sized star at the outer edge of a spiral galaxy. But in spite of their lack of scientific knowledge, in the telling of creation the biblical writers expressed a truth that is timeless. That truth is, we humans did not make the universe, do not own it, and do not control its destiny.

The biblical writers were theologians who conceived that the universe could only be explained as the handiwork of a benevolently purposeful God who was the reference point for all reality. When they introduced Adam into their story, however, they did not portray him as a fellow theologian. They portrayed him rather as a theological innocent. In his original state, Adam knew only that he was *here*, a creature bound to a natural habitat that seemed to be more in favor of his existence than against it.

Decades ago in his book *The American Adam*, R.W.B. Lewis traced the theme of Adam in the American literature of the nineteenth century. Lewis maintained that such seminal American writers as Emerson, Thoreau, and Whitman identified imaginatively with the innocent Adam of Genesis. They aspired to look upon the bright new garden of the American world with eyes that were unclouded by preconceived categories of theological thought. I have often recalled Lewis's book in my reading an English nature writer of the nineteenth century, Richard Jefferies, who lived from 1848–1887. Jefferies is as much an innocent Adam as his American counterparts. But unlike them, he is a writer who is relegated to the margins of literary history.

As a professional writer, Jefferies earned only a modest living for his wife and children. With the noteworthy exception of his novel *Bevis: The Story of a Boy's Life,* Jefferies' fiction did not attract a popular reading public in his own lifetime, nor has it since. To the extent he is remembered today, it is typically for his autobiography and for essays on themes of rural life and nature that were first published in newspapers and journals and later gathered and published under various book titles.

Jefferies was born near the old market town of Swindon, eighty miles west of London in Wiltshire County. The environs in which he grew up were rural. His father was a farmer, but from childhood upward Jefferies had no liking for the practical duties of farming. "He was derided in his father's house," says one of his biographers, "upbraided for idleness and stupidity; considered 'looney' by the neighbors."[6]

Jefferies' reputation for lunacy stemmed from his habit of doing what he liked rather than what others expected of him. He especially liked reading imaginative literature and taking solitary walks in the countryside. During these walks he took minute notice of rural customs and the subtle things of nature. His great gift as a writer was his ability to observe in nature what others might miss or dismiss, and bring to the attention of his readers things remarkable. The following passage, in which Jefferies describes a grain of wheat, is typical of his power of imaginative observation:

If you will look at a grain of wheat you will see that it seems folded up: it has crossed its arms and rolled itself up in a cloak, a fold of which forms a groove, and so gone to sleep. If you look at it some time, . .you can almost trace a miniature human being in the oval of the grain. It is narrow at the top, where the head would be, and broad across the shoulders, and narrow again down towards the feet; a tiny man or woman has wrapped itself round about with a garment and settled to slumber.[7]

He goes further in the passage to suggest that the grain of wheat is "the actual flesh and blood of man." We eat it in the form of bread and it becomes one with us, we with it. "Transubstantiation," he remarks, "is a fact there."[8] This allusion to the Christian doctrine of transubstantiation seems oddly out of place in a passage about a grain of wheat. Jefferies is not suggesting his fidelity to the doctrine, but is parodying it. And this is by no means the single instance in his work where he reveals an unsympathetic attitude toward religious orthodoxy and practice.

In an essay titled "The Country Sunday," in which he draws on memories of his youth, he remarks sardonically on the folk of the Wiltshire countryside who dutifully made their way to church:

The hottest summer day or the coldest winter Sunday made no difference; they tramped through dust, and they tramped through slush and mire; they were pilgrims every week. A grimy real religion, as concrete and as much a fact as a stone wall; a sort of horse's faith going along the furrow unquestioning.[9]

Jefferies himself was temperamentally incapable of "going along the furrow unquestioning." Though imbued in his youth with biblical teachings, in his maturity he reckoned with the Darwinian evolutionary hypothesis that seemed to render obsolete the story of creation contained in the first chapters of Genesis. For him, as for many of his Victorian contemporaries, the Darwinian hypothesis represented a dividing line between an old way of thinking about the world of nature and a new way that had implications for removing any reference to a Creator. W. J. Keith, one of Jefferies' most thorough interpreters, says:

> Jefferies was a man who wanted to believe but could not, who found the empirical approach of science as unsatisfactory as the "high Priori Road" of revealed religion, who considered atheism as illogical as conventional Christianity but was unable to find peace in a vaguely sceptical agnosticism.[10]

In such a state of ambiguity as Keith describes, Jefferies was determined to think about the world of nature without the weight of previous thought—religious or scientific—dictating what *his* thought should be. "Instead of a set of ideas based on tradition," he declared, "let me give the mind a new thought drawn straight from the wondrous present, direct this very hour."[11]

Jefferies' thought about the world of nature is never less bound to previous thought than in his autobiography, *The Story of My heart*, a book that he worked on hit-and-miss over a period of eighteen years before publishing it in 1883. In one of its striking passages, he observes:

> There is nothing human in the whole round of nature. All nature, all the universe that we can see, is absolutely indifferent to us, and except to us human life is of no more value than grass. If the entire human race perished at this hour,

what difference would it make to the earth? What would the earth care? As much for the extinct dodo, or for the fate of the elephant now going.[12]

Behind these words lies a question that Jefferies must have asked himself many times. Could he, on the basis personal familiarity with the world of nature, affirm a Creator who is occupied with the well-being of his creatures? Jefferies had a particular abhorrence of toads. Of the toad, he says in disgust: "All the designless, formless chaos of chance-directed matter, without idea or human plan, squats there embodied in the pathway."[13] To the age-old question of how the world of nature came to be Jefferies had no answer, but he had a sure sense that a benevolently purposeful Creator does not reign over a world where toads exist.

In the autobiography, Jefferies does not describe the course of his life chronologically. It is often not clear if information he offers about a particular event occurred before or after other events that he describes. The book has a random structure that reflects his shifting thoughts over the nearly two decades of its composition. His prime intention is to tell the story of his "heart," a term that he uses interchangeably with the terms *psyche, mind, spirit,* and *soul* to refer to his inner life.

In the opening chapter of the autobiography, Jefferies offers an account of a revelatory experience that occurred to him when he was seventeen years old. One day when his heart was "parched for want of the rain of deep feeling," his "mind arid and dry,"[14] he took a three-mile walk to one of his favorite haunts, a place known among the natives of the Wiltshire countryside as Liddington Hill. "By the time I had reached the summit," he recalls,

I had entirely forgotten the petty circumstances and the annoyances of existence. . . . I was utterly alone with the sun and the earth. Lying down on the grass, I spoke in my soul to the earth, the sun, the air, and the distant sea far beyond. I thought of the earth's firmness—I felt it bear me up; through the grassy couch there came an influence as if I could feel the great earth speaking to me.[15]

He continues:

I hid my face in the grass, I was wholly prostrated, I lost myself in the wrestle, I was rapt and carried away. Becoming calmer, I returned to myself. . . . I did not then define, or analyse, or understand this. I see now that what I laboured for was soul-life, soul-nature, to be exalted, to be full of soul-learning.[16]

Jefferies' account of this experience on Liddington Hill does not contradict his insistence about nature's indifference to humans. What he realizes from his experience, as he explicitly declares, nature is "always within."[17] He does not spell out as a scrupulous thinker might what he means when he says nature is "always within." Instead, he wraps his meaning in language that derives from the vocabulary of religion. In the following passage, he describes his experience when he engages the world of nature in prayer:

I prayed with the glowing clouds of sunrise and the soft light of the first star coming through the violet sky. At night with the stars, according to the season: now with the Pleiades, now with the Swan or burning Sirius, and broad Orion's whole constellation, red Albebaran, Arcturus, and the Northern Crown; with the morning star, the light-bringer, once now and then when I saw it, a white-gold in the violet-purple sky, or framed about with the pale summer vapour floating away as red streaks shot horizontally in the east. . . . All the glory of the sunrise filled me with broader and furnace-like vehemence in prayer.[18]

This is not prayer intended for the hearing of a transcendent God. Neither is it prayer of adoration *to* nature. Prayer for Jefferies is an activity of the heart, in which he brings his whole attention to bear on the appearances of the world of nature. He speaks of "something more subtle than electricity"[19] that he is aware of within himself when he is engaged in the activity of prayer. And after that activity, always came to him the desire, as he records:

That I might be like this; that I might have the inner meaning of the sun, the light, the earth, the trees and grass, translated into some growth of excellence in myself, both of body and mind; greater perfection of physique, greater perfection of mind and soul; that I might be higher in myself.[20]

These words bring closer to understanding what Jefferies means when he says that nature is "always within." He realized that the "inner meaning of the sun" is not in the sun. It is in the human being who brings attention to bear on the beauty and energy of the sun. In turning his face to the sun, in opening his heart to nature's awesome energy, that energy in ways he did not understand entered him and became his own. I imagine that the biblical writers of Genesis could have done no better than Jefferies has done if they had attempted to describe the inner life of Adam at his nativity. When Adam first opened his eyes, it was not God whom he thought of. It was the wonders of the garden itself, which he lacked theological tools to attribute to God.

When Jefferies' publisher asked him to write a description of *The Story of My Heart* that would convey a sense of its contents to the public, he found it impossible to satisfy the request. He had said what he had to say in the way he had to say it, and readers would have to decide for themselves if the book was comprehensible. Afflicted with tuberculosis, Jefferies knew by his mid-thirties that he had little time to live. He published his autobiography under a doomsday edict to sum up insights he had achieved in a life dedicated to observing and writing about the world of nature.

Among his key insights is one he never expresses more directly than in an essay titled "Wild Flowers." In the course of depicting and naming the wild flowers of his native landscape, he registers his frustration at trying to capture the world of nature in words. "It is like a story," he writes, "that cannot be told because he who knows it is tongue-tied and dumb. Motions of hands, wavings and gestures, rudely convey the framework, but the finish is not there."[21] Here Jefferies expresses the insight that nature writing is just that: nature in words. For him, the individual human heart that is open to the world of nature is privy to something *more subtle than electricity* that words cannot convey.

The literary genre of nature writing has assumed a high profile in our environmental age. Books such as Jonathan Bate's *The Song of the Earth*, Lawrence Buell's *The Environmental Imagination*, and John Felstiner's *Can Poetry Save the Earth?* bring to light writers both past and present who think freshly about the world of nature and the human presence within it. Jefferies, to my mind, belongs significantly to the company of such writers.

As far as we can see into cultures of the past, people have told grand stories about the origin and structure of the universe. The theological account of the creation in Genesis is one of these grand stories. Today's grand storytellers tend to be scientists. Jefferies, neither theologian nor scientist, also tells a story of creation, not about how things came to be, but about how things that *are* have registered in his heart. In telling the story of his heart, he advances the truth that the story of the creation is unfinished. The nature writer in every generation is faced anew—as Adam was—with the challenge to find "words and meanings"[22] adequate to the experience of being awake to the awesome energy, on-going life, and the ominous beauty of this material world.

NOTES

1. Prov. 8:29.
2. John Milton, *The Riverside Milton*, ed. Roy Flannigan (Boston: Houghton Mifflin Company, 1998), Book XII, lines 645–49, 710.
3. Rev. 5:13.
4. T. S. Eliot, "East Coker," *Complete Poems and Plays: 1909-1950* (New York: Harcourt, Brace and Company, 1952), 125.
5. Charles Taylor, *A Secular Age* (Cambridge, Massachusetts: Belknap-Harvard University Press, 2007), 327.
6. Henry Williamson, *Richard Jefferies: Selections of his Work with details of his Life and Circumstances, his Death and Immortality* (London: Faber and Faber Limited, 1947), 7.
7. Richard Jefferies, "Walks in the Wheat-Fields," *Field and Hedgerow: Being The Last Essays* (London: Longmans, Green, and Co., 1892), 121.
8. Jefferies, "Walks in the Wheat Fields," 122.
9. Jefferies, "The Country Sunday," *Field and Hedgerow*, 52.
10. W. J. Keith, *Richard Jefferies: A Critical Study* (Toronto: University of Toronto Press, 1965), 81.
11. Richard Jefferies, *The Story of My Heart*, ed. Samuel J. Looker (London: Constable Publishers, 1947), 36.
12. Jefferies, *Story*, 51–52.
13. Jefferies, *Story*, 53.
14. Jefferies, *Story*, 19.
15. Jefferies, *Story*, 20.
16. Jefferies, *Story*, 22.
17. Jefferies, *Story*, 33.
18. Jefferies, *Story*, 26-27.
19. Jefferies, *Story*, 55.

20. Jefferies, *Story*, 60.
21. Richard Jefferies, "Wild Flowers," *The Open Air* (London: Lutterworth Press, 1948), 63.
22. T. S. Eliot, "East Coker," *Complete Poems and Plays*, 125.

2

THE CREATION WITHIN THE GREENHOUSE WORLD OF THEODORE ROETHKE

There was a child went forth every day.

—WALT WHITMAN, "THERE WAS A CHILD
WENT FORTH"

T HE AMERICAN POET Theodore Roethke (1908-1963) was born
in Saginaw, Michigan. His paternal grandfather immigrated to
America in 1897 from East Prussia, where he had been Bismarck's
head forester. In Saginaw, the grandfather started a floriculture business that he passed on to his two sons, Charles and Roethke's father,
Otto. Roethke says of the business:

> When the firm was at its height, around 1920, it took up
> twenty-five acres within the city of Saginaw with a quarter of
> a million feet under glass. We lived in a frame house which
> was in front of the greenhouse and my Uncle Charlie lived in
> a stone house which was next door.[1]

Roethke's acquaintance with the physical world of the greenhouse
came to an end when he was still in his teens. In 1922, Otto and
Charles had a dispute that resulted in their selling the family-owned
business. And in 1925, Roethke left Saginaw to enter the University
of Michigan.

In an essay that he wrote for a rhetoric class as an undergraduate
at the University of Michigan, Roethke spoke of his deep responses
to the world of nature. "I have a genuine love of nature," he said:

> It is not the least bit affected, but an integral and powerful
> part of my life. I know that Cooper is a fraud—that he doesn't
> give a true sense of the sublimity of American scenery. I know
> that Muir and Thoreau and Burroughs speak the truth.
>
> I can sense the moods of nature almost instinctively. Ever
> since I could walk, I have spent as much time as I could in

the open. A perception of nature—no matter how delicate, how subtle, how evanescent,—remains with me forever. I am influenced too much, perhaps, by natural objects. I seem bound by the very room I'm in. I've associated so long with prosaic people that I've dwarfed myself spiritually. When I get alone under an open sky where man isn't too evident,—then I'm tremendously exalted and a thousand vivid ideas and sweet visions flood my consciousness.[2]

These words so typify Roethke's responses to nature that they might well have been written as a postscript to his career. His imagination was heightened by solitude in natural surroundings, "dwarfed" by commerce with persons, a theme reminiscent of nineteenth century Romanticism that influences his poetry from beginning to end. But while Romanticism called attention to the wonders of nature on the surface of the earth, Roethke calls attention to the wonders of nature within the earth itself.

The historian of primitive thought Mircea Eliade speaks of an experience of nature that lingers in the consciousness of modern humanity. He describes this as the mystical experience of autochthony, the profound feeling of having come from the soil, of having been born of the Earth in the same way that the Earth, with her inexhaustible fecundity, gives birth to the rocks, rivers, trees and flowers.[3]

In a sequence of fourteen poems that recall the greenhouse environs of his youth, Roethke creates an imaginative narrative of an autochthonous experience, of both plant and human life growing upward from within the earth's dark mantle. He conveys a sense of this experience in "River Incident," a poem that stands outside the greenhouse sequence.

A shell arched under my toes,
Stirred up a whirl of silt
That riffled round my knees.
Whatever I owed to time
Slowed in my human form;
. . . .
The elements I kept warm
Crumbled and flowed away,
And I knew I had been there before,
In that cold, granitic slime,
In the dark, in the rolling water.[4]

This poem testifies to the poet's profound sense of being a creature of the earth, and it also affords a clue to the experience that is conveyed in the first two poems of the greenhouse sequence.

In the first poem of the greenhouse sequence, "Cuttings," the poet expresses an awareness of the most elemental beginnings of life:

Sticks-in-a-drowse droop over sugary loam,
Their intricate stem-fur dries;
But still the delicate slips keep coaxing up water;
. . . .
One nub of growth
Nudges a sand-crumb loose,
Pokes through a musty sheath
Its pale tendrilous horn.[5]

In the opening line, sticks "drowse" and "droop" as though barely alive. The mere fact of their being in stasis, however, rather than dead, gives the hope of revival. The promise of new life is suggested in the phrases "But still" and "keep coaxing," while the allusion to bulging cells suggests a potential. But this suggestion is followed in stanza two by a suggestion of the obstacles to life being overcome. Before the "One nub: can emerge from the "sugary loam" it must nudge away the "sand crumb." The "musty sheath" must be rent before the young plant can appear, pale and weak in the light of day. This idea of the strain of becoming is continued in "Cuttings (later)":

> This urge, wrestle, resurrection of dry sticks,
> Cut stems struggling to put down feet, . . .
> . . . .
> I can hear, underground, that sucking and sobbing,
> In my veins, in my bones I feel it,—
> The small waters seeping upward,
> The tight grains parting at last.
> When sprouts break out,
> Slippery as fish,
> I quail, lean to beginnings, sheath-wet.[6]

The struggle of the "Cut stems" to "put down feet" or attain "new life" is so fierce that the speaker can only "quail" in its presence. The phenomenon of the "urge" for life is something that not only fascinates but also terrifies him. He "lean[s] to beginnings, sheathe-wet" in the knowledge of the most elementary agonies attending the process of "coming alive," the terrible miracle of growth.

The notion of the struggle and pain of existence is also expressed in "Root Cellar," in which Roethke describes an event in the life of the child-protagonist who is working in the greenhouse. The locus of this event is subterranean:

> Nothing would sleep in that cellar, dank as a ditch,
> Bulbs broke out of boxes hunting for chinks in the dark,

Shoots dangled and dropped,
Lolling obscenely from mildewed crates,
Hung down long yellow evil necks, like tropical snakes.
And what a congress of stinks!—
. . . .
Pulpy stems, rank, silo-rich
Leaf-mold, manure, lime, piled against slippery planks.
Nothing would give up life:
Even the dirt kept breathing a small breath.[7]

Here the image of the mire connotes a condition of life on the level
of the ugly and grotesque. And the image is augmented in "Weed
Puller":

Under the concrete benches,
Hacking at the black hairy roots,—
. . . .
Tugging all day at perverse life:
The indignity of it!—
. . . .
Me down in that fetor of weeds,
Crawling on all fours,
Alive, in a slippery grave.[8]

Both "Root Cellar" and "Weed Puller" hint at a negative meaning of nature, which the protagonist aspires to overcome. He com-
pares himself to an animal, "Crawling on all fours." And they offer
a further commentary on the processes of growth described in
"Cuttings" and "Cuttings (later)." Just as plants must struggle out
of the mire, so must the child-protagonist who is "Alive" but "in a
slippery grave."

At least three other poems in the sequence allude to the negative meaning of nature; "Orchids," "Moss Gathering" and "Child on Top of a Greenhouse." In the first of these, the poet hints at a sinister quality of the tropical orchids:

> They lean over the path,
> Adder-mouthed,
> Swaying close to the face,
> Coming out, soft and deceptive,
> Limp and damp, delicate as a young bird's tongue;
> Their fluttery fledgling lips
> Move slowly,
> Drawing in the warm air.
> . . . .
> Lips neither dead nor alive,
> Loose ghostly mouths
> Breathing.[9]

The funereal aspect of the greenhouse world in "Orchids" is further accentuated in "Moss Gathering." After describing his childhood chore of gathering moss from the marshes for the lining of "cemetery baskets," the poet remembers:

> And afterwards I always felt mean, jogging back over the logging road,
> As if I had broken the natural order of things in that swampland;
> Disturbed some rhythm, old and of vast importance,
> By pulling off flesh from the living planet;
> As if I had committed, against the whole scheme of life, a desecration.[10]

In contrast to the marvelous and reverential presence of the "swampland," the greenhouse has about it something that is strangely foreboding. The poet associates it with threats of danger and death, even in the activity of the child-protagonist at innocent play, as in "Child on Top of a Greenhouse":

> The wind billowing out the seat of my britches,
> My feet crackling splinters of glass and dried putty,
> The half-grown chrysanthemums staring up like accusers,
> Up through the streaked glass, flashing with sunlight,
> . . . .
> A line of elms plunging and tossing like horses,
> And everyone, everyone pointing up and shouting![11]

Though these poems in the greenhouse sequence of which I have spoken stress the negative meaning of nature, the remaining poems in the sequence tend to stress nature's positive meaning. As I have previously mentioned, the poet in 1950 described the greenhouse publicly as "my symbol for the whole of life, a womb, a heaven-on-earth." Some years earlier, however, he wrote in the privacy of his notebooks—which were eventually edited and published under the title *Straw for the Fire:* "What was this greenhouse? It was a jungle and it was a paradise. It was order and disorder. Was it an escape? No, for it was a reality harsher than reality."[12]

A significant feature of Roethke's enthrallment with the greenhouse world is the human presence within it as an ameliorating influence on the jungle-like characteristics of that world. Certainly the theme of human intervention in nature's processes is implied in the poems that focus on the greenhouse workers, those protectors and procreators of the greenhouse who strive to turn its harsh reality into a flowering paradise. "Forcing House," for example, hints at the dynamic role these workers play in the greenhouse as they place the richest nutrients of the mire into the manure machine, to be forced through life-giving pipes to the pulsing plants:

> Vines, tougher than wrists
> And rubber shoots,
> Scums, mildews, smuts along stems,
> . . . .
> All pulse with the knocking pipes
> That drip and sweat,
> . . . .
> Swelling the roots with steam and stench,
> Shooting up lime and dung and ground bones,—
> Fifty summers in motion at once,
> As the live heat billows from pipes and pots.[13]

In this poem, the human presence is felt as the means by which the processes of nature are abetted and speeded until there are "Fifty summers in motion at once."

It is not simply the industry of the workers that Roethke recalls. It is also their empathy with things, which he recalls in at least three poems: "Old Florist," "Transplanting," and "Frau Bauman, Frau Schmidt, and Frau Schwartze." In the first of these poems the reader sees

> That hump of a man bunching chrysanthemums
> Or pinching-back asters, or planting azaleas,
> Tamping and stamping dirt into pots. . . .[14]

And in "Transplanting," the reader stands alongside the poet,

Watching hands transplanting,
Turning and tamping,
Lifting the young plants with two fingers,
Sifting in a palm-full of fresh loam. . . . [15]

"Frau Bauman, Frau Schmidt, and Frau Schwartze" was not included among the Greenhouse Poems as they were published in *The Lost Son and Other Poems* (1949). Roethke later included it in the sequence, however, almost as if to stress the importance of human empathy with nature. Speaking of the women who worked in the greenhouse, he says:

They stood astride pipes,
Their skirts billowing out wide into tents,
Their hands twinkling with wet;
Like witches they flew along rows
Keeping creation at ease;
With a tendril for a needle
They sewed up the air with a stem;
They teased out the seed that the cold kept asleep,—
All the coils, loops, and whorls.
They trellised the sun; they plotted for more than themselves. [16]

The manner in which these women of the greenhouse touch the world is of lasting significance. By their tenderness and delicacy they keep "creation at ease," and by so doing plot "for more than themselves."

To be sure, the life of the greenhouse workers is not without its adversities. The wrists of the "ancient leathery crones" are "thorn-bitten." [17] And the old florist, who patiently fans "life into wilted sweet peas with his hat," or stands "all night watering roses, his feet blue in rubber boots," [18] is a man worn by his labors. The greenhouse is "a reality harsher than reality."[19] But within this reality the human presence is a creative influence that helps nature to realize its fullest productivity and beauty, such as is realized through the human nurturing of carnations, a flower that for Roethke evokes a vision of

> A crisp hyacinthine coolness,
> Like that clear autumnal weather of eternity,
> The windless perpetual morning above a September cloud.[20]

Humans work with what is given in nature. They are not creators in any original sense. There are mysteries of growth within nature in relation to which the human being is no more than an astonished witness. An instance of such growth is suggested in "Flower Dump":

> Cannas shiny as slag,
> Slug-soft stems,
> Whole beds of bloom pitched on a pile,
> Carnations, verbenas, cosmos,
> Molds, weeds, dead leaves,
> Turned-over roots . . . ;
> . . . .
> Everything limp
> But one tulip on top,
> One swaggering head
> Over the dying, the newly dead."[21]

Here in one heap lies the dead and moldering vegetation of the greenhouse, but even this sprouts with the glory of "one tulip." The glory of the tulip belongs essentially to the positive meaning of nature, and it is that meaning the poet expands in "Big Wind."

The first line of "Big Wind" may be taken to be in its literal sense as a question expressing concern about the safety of the greenhouse in a storm. The poet asks: "Where were the greenhouses going?"[22] However, this line may also be taken in a figurative sense as a question about the very structure of existence, of nature's possibility for overcoming its own negative meaning. The first twenty lines of the poem stress the idea of the struggle for survival. The workers strain to keep the pipes supplied with steam; they stuff burlap in holes of the greenhouse to keep out the wind. If elsewhere in the sequence Roethke alludes to the perils of existence within the greenhouse world primarily in relation to the life of the child-protagonist, in this poem he broadens his perception of peril to include the entire world of nature. "Big Wind" expresses the poet's recognitions of how radically the whole of nature is shot through with contingency. This contingency involves all that is transient, chaotic, and discordant in the structure of existence: natural catastrophe, death and anxiety, and all the disparate phenomena of nature. Yet he wants also to speak of a marvelous stoutness in the world that is finally greater than all its contingency, for as he says,

. . . She rode it out,
That old rose-house,
She hove into the teeth of it,
The core and pith of that ugly storm,
Ploughing with her stiff prow,
Bucking into the wind-waves
That broke over the whole of her,
Flailing her sides with spray,
Flinging long strings of wet across the roof-top,
Finally veering, wearing themselves out, merely
Whistling thinly under the wind-vents;

She sailed until the calm morning,
Carrying her full cargo of roses.[23]

The positive meaning of nature is not merely a product of the poet's fancy. It is something that belongs to nature, as is indicated by the ability of the greenhouse to bear her "full cargo of roses" through the storm. The rose was a flower that had special meaning for Roethke. In "The Longing," a poem written toward the end of his career, he declares, "The rose exceeds, the rose exceeds us all."[24] The greenhouse is not a paradise, yet, out of its rich, rank soil emerges the luminous rose. It is as though the poet wants to say, "Who could imagine that?"

Roethke's vision of the creation in the greenhouse sequence of poems is one of human life inextricably bound up with all living matter. Nature, the common mother, gives life from within her to the flora and fauna. But her giving of life presents every living thing with a struggle for survival against disease, decay, and death. It is noteworthy that the greenhouse sails on "until the calm morning" because its keepers have struggled frenetically through the night to the point of physical exhaustion to keep the plants alive. The greenhouse in the sequence is a metaphor for human existence in nature. We do not control nor do we fathom the conditions of life that nature imposes. But it is in our capacity to be life's keepers—a thought worth holding if as a species we would sail into the safety of future mornings.

NOTES

1. Theodore Roethke, *Selected Letters of Theodore Roethke*, ed. Ralph J. Mills Jr. (Seattle, Washington: The University of Washington Press, 1968), 253.
2. Theodore Roethke, *On the Poet and his Craft*, ed. Ralph J. Mills, Jr. (Seattle, Washington: The University of Washington Press), 4.
3. Mircea Eliade, *Myths, Dreams, and Mysteries: The Encounter Between Contemporary Faiths and Archaic Realities* (New York: Harper Torchbooks, Harper and Row, 1960), 164.
4. Theodore Roethke, "River Incident," *The Collected Poems of Theodore Roethke* (New York: Anchor Doubleday, 1975), 47.
5. Roethke, "Cuttings," *Collected Poems*, 35.
6. Roethke, "Cuttings (later)," *Collected Poems*, 35.
7. Roethke, "Root Cellar," *Collected Poems*, 36.
8. Roethke, "Weed Puller," *Collected Poems*, 37.
9. Roethke, "Orchids," *Collected Poems*, 37.
10. Roethke, "Moss Gathering," *Collected Poems*, 38.
11. Roethke, "Child on Top of a Greenhouse," *Collected Poems*, 41.
12. Theodore Roethke, *Straw for the Fire: From the Notebooks, 1943-63*, ed. David Wagoner (New York: Doubleday and Company, Inc., 1972), 150.
13. Roethke, "Forcing House," *Complete Poems*, 36.
14. Roethke, "Old Florist," *Complete Poems*, 40.
15. Roethke, "Transplanting," *Collected Poems*, 40.
16. Roethke, "Frau Bauman, Frau Schmidt, and Frau Schwartze," *Collected Poems*, 42.
17. Roethke, "Frau Bauman, Frau Schmidt, and Frau Schwartze," *Collected Poems*, 42.
18. Roethke, "Old Florist," *Complete Poems*, 40.
19. Roethke, *Straw for the Fire*, 150.
20. Roethke, "Carnations, *Complete Poems*, 41.

21. Roethke, "Flower Dump," *Collected Poems*, 41.
22. Roethke, "Big Wind," *Collected Poems*, 39.
23. Roethke, "Big Wind," *Collected Poems*, 39.
24. Roethke, "The Longing," *Collected Poems*, 182.

3

THE "WILD GOD" OF ROBINSON JEFFERS' STORY OF CREATION

Rolled round in earth's diurnal course,
With rocks, and stones, and trees.

—WILLIAM WORDSWORTH, "A SLUMBER DID MY
SPIRIT SEAL"

IF THERE IS a single poem by Robinson Jeffers that exemplifies his sense of life, it is "Hurt Hawks." It tells of a hawk no longer capable of flight because of its broken wing. The speaker of the poem tries to save the hawk from the cat or coyote that might kill it. For six weeks he feeds the hawk before releasing it to wander "over the foreland hill." But the hawk returns, "asking for death." The speaker says that he gave the hawk "the lead gift in the twilight."¹

The poem tells of only one hawk, but the word "Hawks" is plural. Jeffers generalizes about the condition of living things that struggle, suffer, and die in nature. The poem is in two parts: I and II. In part I, the speaker interrupts his story of the hawk to speak directly to his audience about the "wild God": "You do not know him, you communal people, or you have forgotten him."² The "wild God" is the God Jeffers knew, and tried to make known to others through the medium of his poetry.

Jeffers' father, William Hamilton Jeffers, was a successful Presbyterian clergyman who became a senior professor of biblical thought and language at Western Theological Seminary in Pittsburgh. The father's love of education and travel led the family on trips to Europe where for three years Jeffers attended private schools. By the age of sixteen, when he entered Occidental College in California, he could read, speak, and write in German and French, and through his father's instruction had also acquired knowledge of Greek, Latin, and Hebrew. William Jeffers passed along his commitment to learning to his son, but not his commitment to the Christian faith.

In a poem titled "To His Father," Jeffers writes,

Christ was your lord and captain all your life,
He fails the world but you he did not fail.

"I Father," Jeffers goes on to declare, have "followed other guides."[3] In his following of "other guides," Jeffers not only rejected the idea of Jesus Christ as divine, but also rejected the idea of the creation of the world and humanity's relationship with God as narrated in the creation story of Genesis. In Jeffers' view, the claim in Genesis for humanity's dominion over nature (Gen. 1: 28-31), as well as its alternative claim for humanity's stewardship of nature (Gen. 2:15), were wayward, because both set humanity apart from nature and make humanity subservient to a transcendent God. Jeffers wants to speak for humanity, nature, and God as an inseparable threesome. And that is the way he does speak in the poem "The Unformed Volcanic Earth," in which he invents—as if in opposition to Genesis—his own story of creation. Adhering to Jeffers imagery, I follow his story of creation as it unfolds throughout the poem's 142 lines.[4]

There is no beginning out of nothing. All the ingredients of creation "were here already." In a remote time the earth was a chaos of steaming water and boiling lava. Deep from within the earth's great mass a "female thing" swam to the surface, urged upward by her "lord the sun." This was the primordial mother of life. She was possessed with a "germinal power" which expelled from her womb a "virus" that settled on the warm ocean.

"Time and the world changed." The volcanic storms of the earth and the toxicity of the atmosphere subsided, and the "virus" began to manifest itself. It clung together in bundles of cells, invented chlorophyll, ate sunlight, and erected "far-flung fortifications of being / Against not-being." Somehow, however, there were "assassins" among the bundles of cells that metamorphosed into animals. They discovered it was easier to eat flesh than "feed on lean air and sunlight." When the ocean waters lowered, both plants and animals gravitated to the shores and took up life on land.

Consciousness emerged. "All things are conscious": stones, plants, animals, stars, and galaxies. Humans are especially endowed with consciousness. Their nerves and brains focus consciousness "like a burning glass / To concentrate the heat and make it catch fire." When consciousness catches fire, humans become aware that all of reality makes "one being, one consciousness, one life, one God."

As for the development of humans themselves, the earliest were tree dwellers till "a change of climate killed the great northern forests." Forced down to the ground, humans had to compete with the "Tiger and panther and the horrible fumbling bear and endless wolf packs." Out of fear humans discovered how to use fire and how to invent flint weapons for purposes of defence. They also invented language to celebrate their heroic deeds of survival.

It is the ancient fear of death that makes humans aggressive in their struggle for survival. Human history is red in tooth and claw, a cruel and bloody epic. Attempts of the "great religions of love and kindness" to temper human aggression have had little demonstrated effect. But we should not blame ourselves for being the "Blood-snuffing" creatures that we are. Instead, we should glory in the fact that we are "sense-organs of God." The person who succeeds in identifying himself or herself as "a part of God's life" becomes as "balanced and neutral / As a rock on the shore."

The "wild God" of "Hurt Hawks" is also the God of "The Unformed Volcanic Earth." Jeffers rejects the biblical God who stands above nature as its creator. His "wild God" is nature itself in all its modes, moments, members, appearances, and processes.

In the Foreword to *The Big Sur Coast*—a handsome book of photographs that features lines from Jeffers' poetry—Loren Eiseley tells of his impressions upon meeting Jeffers for the first time:

I felt in his presence almost as if I stood before another and nobler species of man whose moods and ways would remain as inscrutable to me as the ways of the invading Cro-Magnons must have seemed dark to the vanishing Neanderthals. . . . I have never again encountered a man who, in one brief meeting, left me with so strong an impression that I had been speaking with someone out of time, an oracle who would presently withdraw among the nearby stones and pinewood. . . . The sea-beaten coast, the fierce freedom of its hunting hawks, possessed and spoke through him. It was one of the most uncanny and complete relationships between a man and his natural background that I know.[5]

Eiseley describes Jeffers as a person so completely identified with his environment that he seemed virtually to disappear into it. The quality of *disappearance* that Eiseley observed in the man is also in the poetry. Jeffers is earnest in his avoidance of the pathetic fallacy—of imposing personal human values on nature. He goes out of his way to keep from using the pronoun "I." A Jeffers' poem typically begins by focusing on something in nature—a hawk, a mountain, a star—and proceeds as an ego-less meditation on the thing itself. The poetic aim is to draw human consciousness as close to the material world as possible. Indeed, one often senses that Jeffers wants to *be* the thing he is describing, as for instance when he says in "Vulture,"

To be eaten by that beak and become part of him,
to share those wings and those eyes—
What a sublime end of one's body.[6]

In the poem "Autumn Evening," Jeffers insists, "No matter what happens to men . . . the world's well made though."[7] We are here at the heart of Jeffers' doctrine of *inhumanism*, which he described in this way:

It is based on a recognition of the astonishing beauty of things and their living wholeness, and on a rational acceptance of the fact that mankind is neither central nor important in the universe; our vices and blazing crimes are as insignificant as our happiness.[8]

Jeffers does not think well of humanity, and suggests that the planet would be better off if humans had never inhabited it. This attitude is hard to reconcile with the existence of the poetry. Jeffers, after all, is human, and humans are the only creatures on the planet who have the capacity to extol nature in language. His attitude toward humanity is also hard to reconcile with the idea, as it is expressed in "The Unformed Volcanic Earth," that humans are "God's sense organs."[9] If humans did not exist, how would God be conscious of herself? These are conundrums that anybody who reads the poetry thoughtfully must either logically challenge or charitably pass over.

But something that is more worth considering in Jeffers' doctrine of inhumanism than its logical inconsistency is its suggestion that humans accommodate themselves to nature through the pursuit of truth. In the poem "Theory of Truth," he cites three fundamental questions that the pursuit of truth involves.

First, is there a God and of what nature? Second, whether there's anything after we die but worm's meat?
Third, how should men live?[10]

I have indicated how Jeffers answers the first two of these questions, but will briefly amplify. His answer to the first question is yes, there is a God. That God is nature, the impersonal sum of all that is, was, and will ever be. Nature is non-beginning, non-hierarchical, non-moral, and non-ending. His answer to the second question is also yes. When we die we are worm's meat, but the worm itself—to paraphrase a speech in *Hamlet*—is eaten by a fish, which in turn is eaten by a king, who in turn is eaten by a worm. Nature creates us in order to destroy us in order to recreate us in different forms.

Jeffers' answer to the third question—"how men should live?"—is anti-cultural and anti-social. Humans should strive to see beyond the structures of economics, technology, and ideology, which modern society assumes to make up the very fabric of the universe. Human history shows that all such structures are arbitrary, and natural history shows that they are all ephemeral. The day will come when the human species will no longer inhabit the planet. Our species evolved from nature and will devolve into nature. Jeffers seems to draw a sense of religious inspiration from this prospect. In answering the question "how should men live?" he echoes, however unwittingly, the Calvinistic notion that humans should live to celebrate God and enjoy him forever. Jeffers in the poem "Divinely Superfluous Beauty" translates this notion into his own idiom to say that humans should live to acknowledge, celebrate, and enjoy the beauty of the natural world.

> The storm-dances of gulls, the barking game of seals,
> Over and under the ocean . . .
> Divinely superfluous beauty
> Rules the games, presides over destinies, makes trees grow
> And hills tower, waves fall.
> The incredible beauty of joy.[11]

He aspired to celebrate the planet in its wild fecundity, in its mystery, and even in its terror—all of which he declared "Superfluous Beauty."

Jeffers' literary star rose in the 1930s, attained its zenith in the 1940s, and by the time of his death in 1962 had dipped beneath the horizon. The historian of environmentalist literature Lawrence Buell remarks that "after years . . . of neglect Jeffers's poems are beginning to enjoy a certain vogue in today's age of unprecedented environmentalism."[12]

Among contemporary environmentalists who are most like Jeffers in philosophical outlook are advocates of deep ecology. A leading spokesman for this environmental philosophy is the Norwegian philosopher Arne Naess. In his *book Ecology, Community, and Lifestyle*, Naess sketches a set of principles that deep ecology endorses.[13] On the whole, these principles involve three basic insights. *First*, all life, human and non-human, has value in itself. To say that all life has value in itself means that every life form is an end in itself. A tree, for instance, is its own being with its own potentiality, independent of any use a squirrel might make of tree for shelter or a human might make of it as a source of lumber. *Second*, humans at present are far too numerous and have seriously interfered with the richness and diversity of nature's eco-system. A substantial decrease in human population is in order. And *third*, humans must learn to refrain from regarding nature as a collection of resources for their use and enhancement. Humans are co-participants within an ecosystem that when respected permits the flourishing of both human and non-human life.

Embedded in deep ecology is a sensibility that inclines toward Jeffers' doctrine of inhumanism. To quote again from Buell, "No postromantic assault on homocentrism has been more extreme than the 'inhumanism' of Robinson Jeffers."[14] Likewise, no contemporary environmental assault on homocentrism has been more extreme than that of deep ecology. Jeffers' assault on homocentrism, however, is clearly the more extreme. Out of a Calvinistic-like sense of retribution for humanity's spoilage of the natural world, Jeffers would see the presence of our species blotted from the planet. Deep ecology would see the influence of our species on nature's ecosystem appreciably reduced.

Jeffers, as literary prophet of the "wild god," urges his audience to awaken to nature as the fundament of Truth. His personal story of creation says to the audience, open your eyes now, while you can, to the superfluous, sublime, beautiful, intemperate, savage nature that will one day subsume you, and carry you changed into another dimension.

NOTES

1. Robinson Jeffers, "Hurt Hawks," *The Selected Poetry of Robinson Jeffers*, ed. Tim Hunt (Stanford California: Stanford University Press, 2001), 165-66.
2. Jeffers, "Hurt Hawks," *The Selected Poetry*, 165.
3. Jeffers, "To His Father," *Selected Poetry*, 15.
4. Jeffers, "The Unformed Volcanic Earth," *The Selected Poetry*, 689-93.
5. Loren Eiseley, "Foreword," *Not Man Apart: Photographs of the Big Sur Coast, With Lines from Robinson Jeffers*, ed. David Bower (San Francisco: Sierra Club, 1965), 23.
6. Jeffers, "Vulture," *The Selected Poetry*, 697.
7. Jeffers, "Autumn Evening," *The Selected Poetry*, 110.
8. Jeffers, "PREFACE, *The Double Axe and Other Poems*," *The Selected Poetry*, 719.
9. Jeffers, "The Unformed Volcanic Earth," *The Selected Poetry*, 693.
10. Jeffers, "Theory of Truth," *The Selected Poetry*, 547.
11. Jeffers, "Divinely Superfluous Beauty," *The Selected Poetry*, 17.
12. Lawrence Buell, *The Environmental Imagination: Thoreau, Nature Writing, and the Formation of American Culture* (Cambridge, Massachusetts: The Belknap Press of Harvard University Press, 1996), 162.
13. Arne Naess, *Ecology, Community and Lifestyle: Outline of an Ecosophy*, trans. and ed. David Rothenberg (New York: Cambridge University Press, 1995), 29.
14. Buell, *The Environmental Imagination*, 162.

4

"God's in the Dirt": A Letter to Professor E. O. Wilson in an Envelope of Faith

In the sweat of thy face shalt thou eat bread,
till thou return unto the ground; for out of it wast thou taken:
for dust thou art, and unto dust shalt thou return.

—Gen.3: 19

I WAS BORN and reared in a family that held Evangelical Protestant convictions. Regular church attendance, church camps, tent meetings, prayer before each meal, Bible reading, and belief in "born again" experience were all part of my upbringing. My father, who was a jeweler by profession, was also a Methodist layman minister, an inventor, an amateur naturalist, and an avid gardener. There came a time in my liberated adulthood when we had difficulty finding agreement on religious matters. One day, when he was well into his eighties, I was helping him to cultivate his acre of garden. I checked on him regularly to see how he was holding up. Suddenly, he dropped his hoe and gazed at the ground. I was frightened that he was having a heart attack, but no, he was rapt in thought. He turned to me as Moses might have turned to Aaron and said, "God's in the dirt." My father's words live with me, and serve as a backdrop in my reading of E. O. Wilson's book, *The Creation: An Appeal to Save Life on Earth*.

Wilson describes himself as a "secular humanist"[1] who has abandoned the religious faith in which he was reared. As a literary device, he presents the book in the form of a letter to a Southern Baptist pastor, to whom he appeals to join him in an effort to bring religion and science together in the struggle to save life on earth. Wilson writes:

> We have a long way to go to make peace with this planet, and with each other. We took a wrong turn when we launched the Neolithic revolution. We have been trying ever since to ascend *from* Nature instead of *to* Nature. It is not too late for us to come around, without losing the quality of life already gained, in order to receive the deeply fulfilling beneficence of humanity's natural heritage. Surely the reach of religious belief is great enough, and its teachers generous and imaginative enough to encompass this larger truth not adequately expressed in Holy Scripture.[2]

Wilson's letter is one sided; the imaginary pastor has no chance to respond. In the following fabricated, unsent letter, I respond to Professor Wilson in the persona of the pastor.

Dear Professor E. O. Wilson:

When you addressed your book to me in the form of a letter, appealing to me to join you in the effort to save life on earth, I doubt that you expected a letter in return. I hope to offer some correction of your assumptions about my religious views.

You characterize me at the beginning of your letter saying, "You are a literalist interpreter of Christian Holy Scripture. You reject the conclusion of science that mankind evolved from lower forms"[3] I am not as "literalist"[4] in interpretation of Holy Scripture as this characterization suggests. I have absorbed the influences of Darwinian thought, and am confident that the world was not created in six chronological days, and that Homo sapiens did not appear on earth just a few thousand years ago. There is a gap in the Bible between what it says about the creation in literal words and what the words might mean. We are challenged as contemporary interpreters of the biblical story to fill that gap.

The story of the creation in the Bible is multi-layered. The foundational story appears in Genesis, Chapters 1-3. There are two accounts of the creation in these chapters. In the first, Genesis 1: 1-23, God out of a dark watery chaos brings forth light, an overarching heaven, dry land, vegetation, the constellations, living creatures, and finally humans, male and female, which he creates in his own image or likeness. In the course of this six-day activity, God pronounces his creation "good" (1:18). On the seventh day, having completed his creation, God rests.

In the second account, 2: 4-23, God creates man from dust and breathes life into him on the same day that he creates heaven and earth. After he creates vegetation and animal life, he plants a garden in Eden, waters it by four rivers, places man in it, makes animals for man to name, and finally out of a rib taken from man makes woman to be man's companion. Even though these two are differing versions of the creation story in Chapters 1-3 of Genesis, readers traditionally have conflated them and spoken of the two versions as one creation story.

After the creation story that is presented in the first three chapters of Genesis, the Bible turns attention abruptly away from the theme of God's original creation of the world. On the whole, the Bible is an anthropomorphic book. It dwells on the theme of the history and destiny of humanity as conceived under an all-attending Creator. But for all of its anthropomorphism, the Bible does not let us forget that the entire physical creation is continuously under the attendance of the Creator. A striking passage in the Bible that enforces this theme is contained in chapter 8 of Proverbs. In this passage, the Genesis story of creation is recalled and extended. The writer includes Lady Wisdom in the Proverbs version of the creation story. Speaking in her own voice, Lady Wisdom describes the role she has played in the cosmic scheme of creation. I quote her words as they appear in my favorite rendering of them in the King James Version of the Bible.

When *there were* no depths I
was brought forth; when *there were*
no fountains abounding with water.
Before the mountains were settled, before the hills, was I
brought forth:
While as yet he had not made
The earth, nor the fields, nor the
highest part of the dust of the world.

When he prepared the heavens,
I *was* there: when he set a compass
upon the face of the depth:
When he established the clouds
above: when he strengthened the
fountains of the deep:
When he gave to the sea his
decree, that the waters should not
pass his commandment: when he
appointed the foundations of the
earth:
Then I was by him, *as* one
brought up *with him*: and I was
daily *his* delight, rejoicing always
before him;
Rejoicing in the habitable part
of his earth; and my delights *were*
with the sons of men.[5]

The Genesis version of the story of creation focuses on a male
principle of divinity. The Proverbs version of the story of creation
focuses on a female principle of divinity. Both of these principles
are aspects of a single divinity. In the Genesis story, the activity of
the male principle of divinity in creation has been completed, or is
"finished": "Thus the heavens and earth were finished, and all their
multitude."[6] But in the Proverbs story of creation the activity of the
female principle of divinity is not finished. Lady Wisdom's work is
ongoing. She is the principle of divinity in the creation that continues to create.

I have no disagreement with persons who regard the biblical
story of creation in any of its versions as scientifically untenable. The

story that is announced in Genesis and varied in Proverbs is not a scientific treatise, but a sacred story. A scientific treatise proceeds by demonstration. A sacred story proceeds by declaration. Lady Wisdom declares, "Whoso finds me findeth life, and shall obtain favour from the Lord."[7] With these words she urges her listeners to search the creation for themselves, and to enter thoughtfully the spaces that their search opens up to them.

Within the compass of the Bible, there is no greater searcher of the creation than Job. Job has enjoyed an abundant life before things turn against him: his loss of possessions, family, laborers, friends, and health. Driven to despair, Job reflects upon and questions the wisdom of the Creator. Speaking in a voice from out of a whirlwind, the Creator interrogates Job, "Where wast thou when I laid the foundations of the earth?"[8] Then follows in the text—chapters 38 and 39—in the most continuous and compelling nature imagery contained in the Bible, a rehearsal of the wonders of creation that bear witness to the infinite wisdom, power, and watchful care of the Creator over the creation. At the end of the rehearsal of these wonders, Job, now repentant of his original questioning, says, "I have uttered that I understood not; things too wonderful for me, which I knew not."[9]

The Book of Job embodies a declaration that is central to the biblical story of creation. We humans are not the makers of the original nature that gave us birth. Human life, together with every other form of life on earth, owes its origin and development to a wisdom that far surpasses our understanding. Outside my office window here at the parsonage blooms a magnolia tree. Somebody unknown to me planted that tree years ago, but the magnificent thing it has become wondrously exceeds the work of the planter's hands. It seems to have a wisdom of its own, though according to the Book of Job not strictly its own. It derives from the Creator, who has "put wisdom in the inward parts"[10] of all existing things.

"Wisdom" is an image that the Bible gives us to use in our thinking and speaking about the creation. It is striking that in its entire scope the biblical story has nothing to say about humans saving the creation in any autonomous sense. It maintains that the creation is saved independently of humans by the wisdom that originated it, sustains it, and warrants its destiny. The story also maintains, however, that humans have a meaningful role to play in wisdom's unfolding drama of creation.

There are two passages in the Genesis version of the story of creation that declare how humans should play out their role in this unfolding drama. One passage declares that we should "subdue"[11] nature, or use it. The other declares that we should "keep"[12] nature, or care for it. These two passages are not logically contradictory. Nature is on slow time; we modern humans are on fast time. Given the wanton haste with which the swelling human population is currently using nature—plundering its resources, destroying its ecosystems—the day is imaginable when our exhaustive uses of nature will have compromised life on the planet for any fruitful human future. While the meaning of the biblical story of creation is primarily about divine wisdom, it is secondarily about human wisdom. The wise person, in a biblical sense, is one who in the course of using nature takes upon himself or herself the responsibility of caring for nature—of protecting, nurturing, and preserving it—in all its life-filled and life-giving forms.

You say in your letter that in our human struggle to save the creation we need "mentors to trust, heroes to emulate, and accomplishments that are real and enduring."[13] When in 1962 Rachel Carson published her book *Silent Spring*, about the destructive effects of pesticides on the natural world, she dedicated the book to Albert Schweitzer. Principles that Carson greatly admired in Schweitzer are expressed in his autobiography, *Out of My Life and Thought.* In the autobiography, Schweitzer tells of an insight that flashed upon him one evening at sunset while he was traveling up an African river that was populated by a herd of hippopotami. He coined the phrase "Reverence for Life,"[14] which became his guiding principle for conduct. He went on to express the meaning of the phrase in ethical terms: "A man is ethical only when life, as such, is sacred to him, that of plants and animals as that of his fellow-men, and when he devotes himself helpfully to all life that is in need of help."[15]

Schweitzer's principle of reverence for life was prompted by his insight that life is life, whether in a hippopotamus or a human being. On the basis of this insight, he reasoned that life itself is the creation's absolute value. Everything that lives pursues this value in its will-to–live. Schweitzer did not view the creation through rose-colored glasses. He recognized that everything that lives is in competition with the will-to-live in everything else that lives. Big fish eat the little fish, and are in turn eaten by bigger fish. Though he was a thinker of theological depth, he did not attempt to justify the ways of God to man, or offer a theological explanation for why life is accompanied by predation, suffering, and death. Rather, he acknowledged the creation as given in all its conditions, and asked how within his orbit as a human being he could be a positive rather than a negative influence within life's ongoing processes.

In your appeal to me, a pastor, to join you, a scientist, in the struggle to save the creation, you say, "Let us see . . . if we can, and you are willing, to meet on the near side of metaphysics in order to deal with the real world we share."[16] My response is yes, I am willing to meet you on "near side of metaphysics," and I do so on the basis of the biblical story of creation. Each time I read the story, especially as it is rendered in Proverbs and the Book of Job, I am reminded that language about the Creator is not expressed in terms that stretch thought into the beyond, but in terms that direct thought to the physical realities of this world. We may esteem what the Creator is by what the Creator does: that meaning leaps out of the biblical story of creation. And what the Creator has done and continues to do is fill the earth with a wisdom that manifests itself in the myriad forms of life that grace our planet.

The Bible speaks consistently of the heart rather than the mind as the defining center of the human person. One of my favorite quotations from Proverbs is, "Wisdom resteth in the heart of him that hath understanding: but that which is in the midst of fools is made known."[17] Wisdom, in more contemporary language, rests in the hearts of people of common sense, but it has to shout loudly to be heard by fools. It is from within the heart that divine wisdom makes its appeal to human intelligence, affection, and deeds. But if we are to hear wisdom's voice, we must be willing to listen to that voice within us. Are people in the modern world any less capable of hearing wisdom's voice than were people of biblical times? I do not think so. Persons such as Schweitzer and Carson are examples of those among us who can teach us to listen.

I would include you, also, as one who can teach us to listen. Even though you profess that you do not believe in a Creator, your writings about the world of nature, for me, reach beyond your conclusion that "Life was self-assembled by random mutation and natural selection of the codifying molecules."[18] Perhaps life was "self-assembled," but in that case life would be the creator of itself. Is it? I guess our thoughts have to come to rest somewhere in our search for answers about the beginning of life.

Whether or not we agree that there is a Creator, we agree that there is a creation. In your letter, you quote with appreciation words that Darwin wrote in his notebook after he had visited a Brazilian rainforest: "It is not possible to give an adequate idea of the higher feelings of wonder, admiration, and devotion which fill and elevate the mind." In connection with these words, you speak of "Darwin's reverence for life."[19] Is it naïve of me to think that you and I are already joined in the struggle to save the creation by virtue of the principle of reverence for life we share, and which we espouse to others, you in language that is scientific, I in language that is religious?

Respectfully yours,

Pastor Robert Dale

In his autobiography titled *Naturalist*, Wilson devotes a chapter to a description of his religious upbringing that rings true with my own. "One Sunday evening in February 1944" he found "grace" through the experience of baptism. Looking back upon that experience, he writes:

> The still faithful might say I never truly knew grace, never had it; but they would be wrong. The truth is that I found it and abandoned it. In the years following I drifted away from the church, and my attendance became desultory. My heart continued to believe in the light and the way, but increasingly in the abstract, and I looked for grace in some other setting. By the time I entered college at the age of seventeen, I was absorbed in natural history almost to the exclusion of everything else. I was enchanted with science as a means of explaining the physical world, which increasingly seemed to me to be the complete world. In essence, I still longed for grace, but rooted solidly on Earth.[20]

In responding to Professor Wilson in the persona of the pastor, I have offered that the grace or gift of God is a wisdom that manifests itself in, through, and with all living beings. That wisdom, when it calls to us, and we listen, compels a "reverence for life." For what we have reverence, we do not destroy.

NOTES

1. E. O. Wilson, *The Creation: An Appeal to Save Life on Earth* (New York: W. W. Norton and Company, 2006), 3.
2. Wilson, *The Creation*, 13.
3. Wilson, *The Creation*, 3.
4. Wilson, *The Creation*, 3.
5. Prov. 8: 24-31.
6. Gen. 2: 1.
7. Prov. 8: 35.
8. Job, 38: 4.
9. Job, 42: 3−4.
10. Job, 38: 36.
11. Gen. 1: 28.
12. Gen. 2: 15.
13. Wilson, *The Creation*, 138.
14. Albert Schweitzer, *Out of My Life and Thought.* Trans. Antje Bultmann Lemke (Baltimore: The Johns Hopkins University Press, 2009), 155.
15. Schweitzer, *Out of My Life and Thought*, 157−58.
16. Wilson, *The Creation*, 4.
17. Prov. 14: 33.
18. Wilson, *The Creation*, 166.
19. Wilson, *The Creation*, 7.
20. E. O. Wilson, *Naturalist* (Washington, D. C.: Island Press, 1994), 43−44.

5

HARLAN HUBBARD: THE ONE OF CREATION

I went to the woods to live deliberately.

—HENRY DAVID THOREAU, *WALDEN*

Harlan Hubbard was an American painter and writer from Kentucky who over several decades wrote four books, each of which accounts for a period of his life: *Journals, 1929-1944*; *Shantyboat* together with *Shantyboat on the Bayous* (1944-51), and *Payne Hollow* (1952-1973).

I first heard of Harlan Hubbard through a friend, Gene, who was an Indiana State Policeman. As far as was possible, Gene and his wife Lou dedicated themselves to self-sufficient living, building their own house, growing their own food, rearing their family in home-made conditions. They by some means unknown to me were friends of Harlan and Anna Hubbard. One day, during a canoe trip I took with Gene on the Wabash River, he told me of the Hubbards' way of life, and offered to introduce me to them. We would meet in Madison, Indiana, and from there cross the Ohio River to the Kentucky shore to where the Hubbards lived at Payne Hollow. One of the great regrets of my life is that I did not take up Gene's offer. I pleaded at the time that I was busy with other matters. Months later, Gene was killed in a bicycle accident, hit from behind by a drunk driver. I am reminded of an old adage: Do it today for there may be no tomorrow. I owe to Gene that he piqued my curiosity about the Hubbards, and set me on the path to learning about them.

Harlan Hubbard was born in 1900 in the town of Bellevue, Kentucky, across the Ohio River from Cincinnati. He was the third and last child of Rose and Frank Hubbard, who maintained their modest household on the father's earnings as a house painter and wallpaper hanger. The father died of a stroke when Hubbard was only seven. To help support the family, the two older boys, Frank and Lucien, went to work for a newspaper in Cincinnati. But after a few years they found work in New York City and persuaded their mother to join them there.

At the time of this move, Hubbard, who was fifteen, did not want to leave his familiar surroundings. Once he and his mother had moved to the Bronx area of New York, however, Hubbard made the most of the cultural and educational advantages the metropolis offered. His chief pastimes—when he was not attending high school or working at the delivery of groceries—were walking the shoreline of the Harlem River, strolling city parks and the Bronx Zoo, visiting museums, libraries, and attending art exhibits and concerts. As a high school student, he excelled in the study of languages, German and Latin, and graduated with honors in 1918. His mother was keen on his attending Cornell, but he chose instead to study art at the National Academy of Design School.

Before his enrollment in art school at age nineteen, Hubbard had worked for two summers in upstate New York through a government program that supplied farm workers during the years of the First World War. Coincident with this farm work, he discovered in 1918 a copy of Thoreau's *Walden* in a public library. Hubbard writes:

> I . . . stumbled on Thoreau in a branch library. The reading of *Walden* and the farm constituted an introduction to nature which gave me a new direction. This did not interfere with my going to art school in the city, but the desire for a wilder life became an undercurrent.[1]

For Hubbard, the discovery of Thoreau was a seminal life experience. From the time of that discovery to the time of his death in 1988, he regarded Thoreau as his chief spiritual guide.

In 1921, Hubbard left art school and accompanied his mother back to Kentucky. But instead of returning to Bellevue, they settled farther up the Ohio River in the town of Fort Thomas. Hubbard took a job as a day laborer for a local contractor and became skilled in carpentry and masonry. Then, in 1923, he designed and built a house on a town lot where he and his mother lived together till her death in 1943.

Hubbard was attentive to his mother, and speaks respectfully of her in his *Journals*. But their relationship had its ups and downs. Rose Hubbard was a practical woman who desired for her son a more conventional life than he was disposed to follow. Instead of trying to get ahead in the world, Hubbard, when he was not employed at day labor, sketched and painted, made woodblock prints, roamed the countryside, explored the Ohio River by canoe and johnboat, talked with river people, played his violin, wrote in his journals, and longed for a "wilder life."[2]

Thoreau had lived at Walden Pond for just over two years, from 1845 to 1847. "Why," Hubbard asked, "did not Thoreau go farther, quit playing at this natural life, throw aside life in this world entirely and live as nearly as he could a life conforming with 'nature'?"[3] In asking himself this question, Hubbard was setting the course for his future.

In 1943, he married Anna Eikenhout, a librarian at the Cincinnati Public Library, who encouraged him to fulfill his dream of building a shantyboat and drifting down the Ohio River to the Mississippi, and down the Mississippi to New Orleans. They fulfilled this dream, taking nearly seven years to complete a river journey that they extended into the bayou country of the Mississippi Delta. At the journey's conclusion, they sold the shantyboat and bought seven acres on the banks of the Ohio River in Trimble County, Kentucky, nine miles below Madison, Indiana. At Payne Hollow, the site of an old riverboat landing, they built a rustic house, and for over three decades—without utilities, telephone, or other conventions of modern living—lived on what Hubbard liked to call "the fringe of society."[4]

Hubbard claimed that in separating himself from society he had no theories to prove. In *Shantyboat*, he writes:

I merely wanted to try living by my own hands, independent as far as possible from a system of division of labor in which the participant loses most of the pleasure of making and growing things for himself. I wanted to bring in my own fuel and smell its sweet smoke as it burned on the hearth I had made. I wanted to grow my own food, catch it in the river, or forage after it. In short, I wanted to do as much as I could for myself, because I had already realized from partial experience the inexpressible joy of so doing.[5]

One of the things I find refreshing about Hubbard is that he offered no theoretical plans for saving nature. Like Thoreau, he went to the woods to live deliberately, not to save the woods. Yet, if more people in contemporary society had Hubbard's sense of respect for nature there would be less need for talk of saving it. Hubbard walked the earth thoughtfully and humbly. In that, he was an important environmental example. He objected that modern cities and suburbs had extended too far into the countryside; that the automobile and highway had taken pleasure out of travel; and that technological gadgets and labor-saving devices had robbed people of self-reliance. At the conclusion of *Payne Hollow*, he frames his ideal landscape as a "rural countryside" of "meadows and croplands" with "the habitations of men in the distance and the effects of their innocent work to be seen here and there."[6] This is Hubbard's ideal of American landscape when it was primarily agrarian, before it was cluttered with people, generic houses, high tension lines, and belching smokestacks.

Unlike the Luddites, who rejected the Industrial Revolution, Hubbard acknowledged that the Industrial Revolution had brought benefits to people's lives. He even expressed satisfaction at some of its mechanical inventions, as when he remarks, "A stern wheel is the most fascinating piece of machinery I've ever seen."[7] He wished, nonetheless, that the Industrial Revolution had somehow stopped short of the twentieth century. Hubbard tried, and in large measure succeeded, to live by a nineteenth century agrarian ethos in a twentieth century mechanized and urbanized world.

In the 1990s, my wife Freda and I decided to take a week to find Payne Hollow and to explore the country that surrounds it. I am not aware of the physical condition of Payne Hollow today, or of who owns it. An entry I made in my journal two decades back, however, gives directions to Payne Hollow, and preserves our experience of having visited there.

A Day at Payne Hollow

Payne Hollow is an old boat landing on the Kentucky side of the Ohio River. A few miles upriver on the Indiana side is the village of Hanover. The Hubbards used to row their johnboat a half-mile across the river from their place on the Kentucky side to the Indiana side to pick up their mail, or to ferry back and forth friends and curiosity seekers who came to visit them.

There are no signs to Payne Hollow. The surest way to get there is from the Kentucky side. Go to the village of Milton, Kentucky, make your way for about five miles on the paved road that leads westward, then ask a local resident for final directions. At the end of a lane that leads off a gravel road, you come to an opening in the woods. This is the beginning of the precipitous descent you must make by foot. The rutted, rocky path drops four hundred feet in a mile. At the end of that mile, you cross a creek. At the top of the slope across the creek is an old farm bell raised a couple of feet off the ground. We rang it and waited. The current owner responded by ringing a bell mounted outside the Hubbard house. He greeted and invited us to inside the house.

The house sits on a rise that is maybe forty feet above the river level, whose shore is a mere hundred yards away. Below the house is a garden plot that Hubbard planted every year after the spring floods. He also planted a garden along the ridge above the house that leads to the goat shack. The goat shack itself, because of the erosion of the shoreline, is doomed to collapse into the river. Indeed, the whole property is threatened. "A river tugs at whatever is within reach," Hubbard wrote, "trying to set it afloat and carry it downstream."[8] He reflected on the prospect that Payne Hollow itself would one day be swallowed by the river.

The house, which is basically one large room, is maintained. The polished sycamore-wood floor that Hubbard shaped and sanded out of rough lumber gives off a sheen from the light coming through an expansive multi-paned window. From the window you can see down to the river through foliage of trees. We sat with the owner before the window. Miracles of light played on the river's surface, while he told stories of the Hubbards' way of life on the fringe of society.

Hubbard had an attitude of taking life as it comes, of not worrying about tomorrow, in the certainty that in the end something would turn up that would help him to deal with any problem at hand. This attitude served him well in his ongoing struggle against the imperatives of the consumer culture. Hubbard was fond of saying "whatever we need is at hand."[9] He was the complete improviser, do-it-yourselfer, scavenger of cast-off materials.

One day he went rummaging in a town dump for materials that he might use in building the shantyboat. For weeks he had thought about the kind of stove he could place in the shantyboat. His eye fell on the "oblong tank, more than two feet in length." For "no reason at all," he writes, the tank "suggested a fireplace to me." In considerable detail, he explains how he lugged the tank back to the shantyboat, hammered it into an aesthetically pleasing shape, cut a hole for the pipe, and mounted it on bricks. He concludes the episode by saying: "Most gratifying it was to sit inside on cool nights and mornings with a blaze on our hearth."[10] Such passages are abundant in Hubbard's writings. They show a man constantly looking for possibilities of utility, beauty, and pleasure in the seemingly useless junk of a throw-away society. Like Thoreau, Hubbard made himself relatively independent of material things by limiting his material demands. And he had an uncanny knack for meeting those demands from whatever was at hand.

Life on the fringe would have been much less accommodating for the Hubbards had it not been for Anna's cultured ways, which provided a balance to Hubbard's roughcast ways. She graduated from The Ohio State University with honors in 1925, then went on to teach German and French for a few years at Hope College in Michigan.[11] At the time Hubbard met her, perhaps in the late 1930s, she was working as a librarian in the Fine Arts Department of the Cincinnati Public Library. In his writings, Hubbard guards the story of their courtship and marriage as though he wants it to belong only to them. He is unstinting in his praise of her, however, as the source of fastidiousness in the life they enjoyed together.

From her Dutch ancestors, Anna had inherited an old world sense of order and decorum, which she brought to bear in all aspects of her homemaking. Hubbard never ceased to admire her minute attention to their domestic surroundings. He also admired her inventiveness as a cook. They did as little buying from the grocery as possible. They relied on garden products; fish from the river; herbs and berries from the woods; goods they had canned and stored in the cellar beneath the house; and on the milk and meat of their goats. Even the occasional groundhog was part of their diet. Anna prepared delicious meals, and served them formally on blue and white china dishes.

In addition to her qualities as a homemaker, Anna was an accomplished cellist and pianist. When they settled at Payne Hollow, the Hubbards acquired the Steinway grand piano that had been in the home of Anna's parents, and proudly established it as the focal point of their home. They played classical duets, she playing the piano or cello, he the violin or viola. The rich tones they made filled "the hollow to the brim and [reached] the far shore through the open windows."[12] Along with regularly making music, the Hubbards read aloud from thought-provoking books.

Hubbard said that everything he and Anna did together derived its vitality and significance from their contrasting natures of "roughness and refinement." He goes on to say, "Beneath the surface...was an underlying ground of sympathy between us which reconciled our diversity."[13] People who knew the Hubbards noted how they seemed oddly, but rightly, suited to one another, as though two individuals had found the formula for blending their contrasting natures into one.

Whether as a shantyboater or a homesteader, Hubbard liked to think of himself as a riverman, though he admitted that in comparison with "a genuine riverman, one who was 'born in a johnboat with the catfish,'"[14] he was only an amateur. Insofar as he thought of himself as being a professional at anything, it was as an artist. Over the course of his life he created hundreds of paintings and woodblock prints that had no wide viewing public. Today, many of his art works are in the possession of private collectors, as well as of various public institutions. The University Press of Kentucky publishes *The Woodcuts of Harlan Hubbard.* Wendell Berry's biography, *Harlan Hubbard: Life and Work,* features a painting of Hubbard's on its cover, as does the dust jacket of his novel *Jayber Crow.* The book cover of *Great Possessions,* by the Amish nature writer David Kline, also features a painting of Hubbard's. In death, Hubbard as an artist has attained a degree of visibility and appreciation that eluded him in life.

The vision of the river world that Hubbard renders in his writings he also renders in his paintings. He delighted in creating paintings of dilapidated riverfront buildings, long river views with human habitations in the fore or background, shantyboats and steamboats, contoured farmlands, deserted streets of river towns, and woodland scenes. In these paintings he often inserts human forms, but not in a way that they force themselves on the viewer's eye. It is as though the painter wants the viewer to discover these forms for himself or herself, diffused among the colors. Humans have their place in Hubbard's paintings not as the center of attention, but as part of something much larger. He consistently points beyond the human world to the background of nature that enfolds the human world.

There is a religious sense of life consistently present in Hubbard's writings and paintings. He was not religious in a church-going way, but he often spoke of "faith." He writes:

> Much as I admire the Christian principles and teaching, and the people . . . who follow them, for myself, I require a more direct revelation, not one that must come through so many minds before it reaches mine. I must have a faith that I can see and hear, one that I can feel without thinking or even trying to put it into words. It is not for anyone else, it is a personal faith.[15]

The object of Hubbard's "personal faith" was the river. In its physical presence he found value beyond all price. It provided food for his physical needs; friendship from among the shantyboaters and rural people who lived along its shores; gratifying work; educational experience; aesthetic pleasure; and a glimpse into the very heart of creation. Just as Emerson spoke of the Oversoul and Thoreau of the

Bottomless Pond, so Hubbard spoke of the River. In each of these writers, their chosen symbols acclaim an awesome and benevolent Power that is within nature.

In a journal entry, Hubbard writes:

> To arise in the frosty morning at the point of daybreak, climb the hill and cut wood while the sky lightens above the soaring trees; to eat this wholesome, sweet food, to use my body, hands and mind at the endless work I have to do; to read by the firelight, to sleep warm and snug; all this shared by my loving partner—what manner of a man originated this idea of a happier life beyond death.[16]

For Hubbard, there was no happier life beyond death than being on the river. He did sometimes have intimations of immortality beyond the grave, but he did not necessarily trust them. What he was certain of was "the One who made the river and set it flowing."[17] In that One he put his faith, and found joy.

NOTES

1. Harlan Hubbard, *Journals 1929-1944,* eds. Vincent Kohler and David F. Ward (Lexington, Kentucky: The University of Kentucky Press, 1987), 5.

2. Hubbard, *Journals,* 5.

3. Hubbard, *Journals,* 24.

4. Hubbard, *Journals,* 15.

5. Harlan Hubbard, *Shantyboat: A River Way of Life* (Lexington, Kentucky: The University of Kentucky Press, 1953), 38.

6. Harlan Hubbard, *Payne Hollow: Life on the Fringe of Society* (Frankfort, Kentucky: Gnomen Press, 1974), 166.

7. Hubbard, *Journals,* 132.

8. Hubbard, *Shantyboat,* 1.

9. Hubbard, *Journals,* 71.

10. Hubbard, *Shantyboat,* 14–15.

11. Wendell Berry. *Harlan Hubbard: Life and Work* (New York: Pantheon Books, 1990), 4.

12. Hubbard, *Payne Hollow,* 80.

13. Hubbard, *Payne Hollow,* 35–36.

14. Hubbard, *Shantyboat,* 48.

15. Harlan Hubbard, *Payne Hollow Journal,* ed. Don Wallis, with illustrations by the author (Lexington, Kentucky: The University Press of Kentucky, 1996), 90.

16. Hubbard, *Payne Hollow Journal,* 154.

17. Hubbard, *Shantyboat,* 74.

6

WENDELL BERRY: WEEPING PROPHET OF HOPE

I brought you into a plentiful land to eat its fruits
and its good things.
But when you entered you defiled my land.

—JEREMIAH 2:7

THE NARRATOR IN J. Hector St. John De Crèvecoeur's *Letters From An American Farmer* (1782) portrays himself as James, an artless farmer, who dabbles in literary matters. In this guise of a rustic, Crèvecoeur created one of the classics of nature writing in American literature. All nature writing points to the physical world, but some, like the *Letters*, points specifically to features of the physical world that are a fusion of human labor and nature's spontaneous processes. This kind of nature writing is "agrarian" writing, and Wendell Berry is a prominent representative of the genre among contemporary American writers.

In a literary career of over half a century, Berry has continuously concerned himself with the passing of a traditional agrarian way of life within American society. A skillful polemicist, he challenges the American lust for industrial, technological, and economic development. American society owes its health, Berry maintains, to its agrarian roots. To the extent we neglect this truth we neglect the values of independence, self-reliance, diligence, simplicity, and thrift that were seminal to America as a young nation.

Knowledge alone, in Berry's view, will not restore our health, or waken us to our agrarian roots, nor will ethics, for by themselves they do not arouse motivation strong enough to transform the exploitative economic patterns to which we have become accustomed. Berry contends that the best hope for transforming these patterns lies in the spiritual resources of religion.

In a talk titled "Christianity and the Survival of Creation"[1] that he gave at the Southern Baptist Theological Seminary in Louisville, Kentucky, Berry complained that most Christians do not know how to understand the Bible in light of the story of creation. The proof is in behavior. If Christians did know how to understand this story they would not be so eager to join the rest of society in the destruction of the natural world. What the story essentially teaches, Berry pointed out, is twofold: that we humans do not own the world; and that on this earth we are merely guests and stewards of a Divine Economy—the realm of nature that divinity originally provided for our well-being. One can only guess what affect Berry's talk might have had on the clerics who were in his audience when they next mounted the pulpit to preach to their congregations. He himself demonstrates throughout his work that he is a careful student of the Bible, and that the story of creation is central to his literary vision.

In Genesis 1-3, the story of humanity's relationship to the natural world unfolds in three sequential images. We were born into an environmentally provident Eden. This was the Garden of Paradise. Through our willfulness we violated the conditions for remaining in the Garden. This was the Fall. We were excluded from the Garden to face the future. This was the Judgment. I think of Berry's work overall in light of these three biblical images.

THE IMAGE OF PARADISE

Berry imagines the Creation as it originally sustained our first parents in the Garden. Every loved and placid landscape was fertile, yielding fruits to the mere touch of the hand. Adam and Eve lived in such a way that they took nothing more from nature's storehouse than they needed for the day. But they were excluded from the Garden, and ever after lived east of Eden earning bread by the sweat of their brow.

Though the original Garden is behind us, the ideal of it remains deeply imbedded in human consciousness. Writing about a walk he has taken in the flowering woods on a spring day, Berry speaks of

The forfeit Garden that recalls
Itself here, where both we and it
Belong.[2]

According to this way of thinking, the current world of nature offers reminders of that "forfeit Garden." It is sad we lost it. Still, there is promise in the ongoing beauty and fertility of nature that what we have lost we can in some measure reclaim if we can adopt ways of stewardship that honor nature rather than violate it.

Berry's conception of stewardship involves the notion that humans should be companions to nature not only in the practices of farming but also in the "use and care of created things"[3] in general. He has a private list of persons whom he admires for their "competent and loving human stewardship of the earth."[4] At the head of this list is Thomas Jefferson, whom he regards as the chief agrarian architect in the history of American society. The list also includes, among Berry's contemporaries, Harry Caudill, Wes Jackson, and Gene Logsdon. But the persons whose stewardship Berry has commemorated most personally in his work are Harlan and Anna Hubbard.

In a biography titled *Harland Hubbard: Life and Work*, Berry tells how he first met the Hubbards. During a trip by canoe down the Ohio River, Berry and his companion were in need of drinking water when they saw a clearing along the embankment and the gable of a house sticking up in the background. Having paddled ashore, they climbed a path that led to the house. There, a "lean, gray-haired man, darkly suntanned wearing only a pair of pants was sitting on the terrace, talking with some guests."[5] Berry and his companion asked the man if he could spare some water to fill their water keg. "He directed us courteously and with few words," Berry writes, "to the door of the house," with instructions to "ask his wife if she could spare us some water."[6] Harlan's wife, Anna, was a graciously reserved woman who seemed she would have felt more at home in a Victorian mansion than in a rustic house on a riverbank. Anna obligingly filled the water keg, gave the canoeists tomatoes for their supper, and told them where thy might camp for the night just below the mouth of a nearby creek. This occasion was the beginning of a friendship between Berry and the Hubbards that lasted from 1964 to the time of their deaths, Anna's in 1986 and Harlan's in 1988. Recalling his impressions on that first of his many visits to the Hubbard homestead, Berry says that he was struck by how carefully the Hubbard's paid attention to their environment:

> Everything they had done there had about it an implicit respect for the place. The buildings had been placed and the gardens laid out in such a way as to do no damage to the landscape.
>
> It was a difficult site for a homestead, one that would not last well under hard or careless use, but these people were not doing anything there that they could not keep on doing forever, if they lived long enough.[7]

In the Hubbards, Berry had discovered two persons in twentieth-century America whose companionship with nature was a conscientious, consistent, and rewarding way of life.

Berry's biography is about the Hubbards but at the same time about himself. It is his testimony to a vision of the creation and to a life of stewardship that vision compels. We humans are not the rulers of the creation, as enthusiasts of industrial, technological, and economic development tend to imagine. We *do* have the greatest potential of all creatures for communion with nature. To realize that communion is to enter into the mystery of a Divine Economy wherein the Creator loves nature, gives to it, and gives to us through it. The life of stewardship—as Berry renders it through his portrait of the Hubbards—is acknowledging our place in the order of the creation as grateful recipients, intelligent users, and dutiful caretakers of nature's garden.

THE IMAGE OF THE FALL

In his book *The Unsettling of America,* Berry gives a gloomy account of how historically American society has failed in its stewardship of nature's garden. Jefferson was right, Berry maintains, in his agrarian design for an American landscape of woods, meadows, orchards, and croplands, with free family farms and close-knit rural communities. Instead, what America has become is an overpopulated landscape cluttered with cities, generic suburbs, redundant roadways, high-tension lines, and land-devouring commercial and industrial enterprises. Under a materialistic economics dedicated to the pursuit of convenience, products, and profit, we have forgotten the Divine Economy and lived profligately and ruinously on the land. In Berry's own words, "We are fallen."[8]

The image of a fallen humanity in a fallen landscape is never far beneath the surface in either Berry's essays or his fiction. His fiction consists primarily of a series of novels and short stories about Port William, an imaginary community that is modeled after the community of Port Royal where Berry grew up in the burly tobacco-growing region of north-central Kentucky. In these narratives—for all the warm-hearted feeling they contain—Berry is not imagining a rural community that has resisted the intrusions of modern society. Rather, he is imagining a community that has been affected by those intrusions, and bit-by-bit has accommodated itself to the materialistic economics that have overwhelmed the Jeffersonian ideal of an agrarian society. Port William is Berry's rural window on the moral and spiritual condition of American society at large.

If we read the novels and short stories about Port William in their order of publication, that order is: *Nathan Coulter,* 1960 (novel), *A Place on Earth,* 1967 (novel), *The Memory of Old Jack,* 1974 (novel), *The Wild Birds,* 1986 (short stories), *Remembering,* 1988 (novel), *Fidelity,* 1992 (short stories), *A World Lost,* 1996 (novel), *Jayber Crow,* 2000 (novel), *Hannah Coulter*, 2004 (novel), and *Andy Catlett*, 2006 (novel). The pivotal work in this series is *The Memory of old Jack*. Here we meet most of the characters who live either in the community of Port William—population about 100—or within its rural environs, and see as for back into the history of the community as Berry pursues it.

The Memory of Old Jack is told in flashbacks from the viewpoint of a ninety-two year old farmer. In 1952, Jack Beechum, his farming days behind him, is living at Mrs. Hendrick's run-down boarding house in Port William. When he was four, his two older brothers had gone off to the Civil War, from which they never returned. Upon the death of both parents, Jack's sister, Nancy, reared him. After an eleven-year courtship, Nancy married a successful local farmer, Ben Feltner. By then Jack was nineteen and old enough to be independent. With Ben's financial backing, Jack bought the neglected and depleted farm of 150 acres that had belonged to his parents, and little by little repaired the old house, built fences, and reclaimed the land.

When Jack was approaching thirty, he met Ruth Lightwood at a church service, fell in love with her good looks, and married her. The marriage, writes Berry, "was the great disaster of both their lives."[9] Ruth, who came from a comfortable background, wanted more out of life than the social isolation and hard work that farm life provided. To raise himself in Ruth's esteem, to persuade her that after all he had large ambitions, Jack decided to extend his land ownership by buying the neighboring Farrier Place and surprising Ruth with its purchase. Ruth was surprised and pleased. She now had "a vision of Jack as a man on horseback, overseeing the work of other men."[10]

After three years, though, Jack had a falling out with his African-American sharecropper, Will Wells, and had to sell the Farrier Place because he could not keep it up on his own. This jolt of selling the Farrier Place, together with the death of their second child, affected the marriage with a coldness neither Jack nor Ruth could overcome, though they continued to live under the same roof. After several years, Ruth, fallen deathly ill, went to Louisville to spend her last days with their daughter Clara and Clara's wealthy banker husband Gladstone Petitt.

Ruth has been dead seventeen years when the novel opens, and Jack, reflecting on the past, is remorseful over the ways he failed Ruth as a husband. The story that Berry tells of their relationship is of an agonized marriage. Looking at the novel from an agrarian perspective, however, it is not Jack and Ruth's marriage that is at the center. It is rather Jack's misdirected ambition.

Berry's account of Jack's desire to own more land recalls Tolstoy's story titled "How Much Land Does a Man Need?"[11] about a peasant farmer who was eager to impress his relatives and neighbors with his worth. Hearing of an area beyond the Volga where he could buy fertile land cheaply, he set out. When he reached the area, the leader of a farming village offered to sell him for 1000 rubles as much land as he could walk around between sunrise and sunset. At the end of the day he had successfully encircled many miles from his point of departure, only to drop dead from exertion at that same point upon his return. "How much Land Does a Man Need?" Tolstoy asks in his title—only enough land to bury him in.

The peasant farmer's ambition in Tolstoy's story is also Jack's. And Jack's ambition, from Berry's angle, foretells farming's increasingly abstract relationship with the natural world since before the beginning of the twentieth century. In the course of the novel, Jack overcomes his ambition to own more land, and concentrates on making his 150 acres into something contained, productive, and enduring that he could pass to a successor. But not before he had brought near ruin to himself by yielding to the endemic American belief that more is better. Berry portrays Jack as a farmer who straddles a dividing line between two ways of thinking about farming in America: an old way that values restraint, is labor intensive, and stresses cooperation with nature; and a new way that values expansion, is mechanized, and stresses control of nature. At the end of the novel, after Jack has died, several of the characters are gathered in the stripping room of Jack's barn. While working the tobacco, they remember Jack by recalling some of his pithy expressions:

"I know what a man can do in a day."
"If you're going to talk to me, you'll have to walk."
"Ready *hell*! I *been* ready!"[12]

Berry closes the novel with the words: "They know that his memory holds them in common knowledge and common loss. The like of him will not soon live again in this world, and they will not forget him."[13] The death of Old Jack marks the end of a farming era that twentieth century industrial farming steadily swept from America's cultural imagination.

One of the characters gathered in the stripping room of Jack's barn at the conclusion of *The Memory of Old Jack* is Andy Catlitt, a distant relative of Jack's who is home from college for the holidays. Andy might be a persona for Berry himself. At least Andy's story of leaving the community to go to college, then after much wandering and soul searching returning to the community to take up farming, resembles the pattern of Berry's own life.

In 1977, Berry debated Earl L. Butz at Manchester College in North Manchester, Indiana. Butz, as Secretary of Agriculture under the Nixon administration, held agrarian views that have had continuing effects on farming in America to this day. According to those views, there are too many farmers; small family farms are inefficient; food is a tool of war and trade; and farmers need to get bigger or get out of farming. Butz was purposeful in advancing what is now called the "agribusiness" of farming "in larger monocultures on larger holdings with fewer farmers, [with] larger and more expensive machines, [and] more chemicals."[14] Butz stood for virtually everything in agrarianism that Berry stood against. In the debate, they simply talked past one another.

The debate stuck in Berry's memory. Years later he revisited it in his novel *Remembering*. Andy Catlett, after graduating from college, worked as an agriculture journalist first in San Francisco then in Chicago. He married his college girlfriend, Flora, and they had two children. After several years of living in cities and practicing agricultural journalism, Andy and his family moved from Chicago back to Port William, where they bought the deserted and overgrown Harford Place. Andy, now about forty years old, settled into the life of a marginal farmer until he lost his right hand in a corn picker. Andy fell into dejection and argued with Flora over trifles.

The novel opens a few months after Andy has lost his hand. Apparently he had established a good reputation during his career as a journalist, for he received an invitation to speak at a Midwestern agricultural conference. The tone of the conference was set by a "high official" who said that as a result of industrial farming "Millions of people have been freed from groveling in the earth so that they can now pursue the finer things in life."[15] Stirred by this remark and similar ones by a succession of academic speakers who preceded him, Andy, when he reached the podium, abandoned his prepared speech and launched into a tirade against the intellectualizing and industrializing of farming:

No farmer is here. No farmer has been mentioned. No one who has spoken this morning has worked a day on an actual farm in twenty years, and the reason for that is that none of the speakers wants to work on the farm or to be a farmer.

The real interest of this meeting is in the academic careerism and the politics and the industrialism of agriculture.[16]

This episode in the novel represents one of Berry's responses to Butz's agrarian views. A second response comes in an episode where Andy, during his career as a journalist, had gone to Ohio to interview "that year's Premier Farmer,"[17] Bill Meikelberger. The episode is pure satire. Of Meikelberger, Berry writes:

He farmed two thousand acres he had acquired by patiently buying out his neighbors in the years since his graduation from the college of agriculture at Ohio State. He was the fulfillment of the dreams of his more progressive professors. On all the two thousand acres there was not a fence, not an animal, not a woodlot, not a tree, not a garden. The whole place was planted in corn, right up to the walls of the two or three unused barns that were still standing. Meikelberger owned a herd of machines. His grain bins covered acres. He had an office like a bank president's.[18]

In addition, Meikelberger had ulcers, huge debts, and his wife worked at a job in town to help make ends meet. Meikelberger is Berry's prototype of the industrial farmer, and from Berry's standpoint the antithesis of what a farmer ought to be.

In contrast to Meikelberger, Berry describes an Amish Farmer named Isaac Troyer whom Andy also interviewed during his career as a journalist. When Andy looked around Troyer's eighty-acre farm,

He saw that the buildings were painted and in good repair. He saw the garden, newly worked and partly planted behind the house. He saw the martin boxes by the garden, and the small orchard with beehives under the trees. He saw fifteen guernsey cows and two . . . black mares in a pasture. He saw a stallion in a paddock beside the barn, and behind the barn a pen from which he could hear the sound of pigs. He saw hens scratching in a large poultry yard. Now and then he could hear the voices of children.[19]

Troyer and his family were healthy, debt free, and they did not work on Sunday. The difference between Meikelberger and Troyer is the difference between an industrial farmer who has only an abstract economic relationship with the land and a true farmer who has an intimate physical and spiritual relationship with it.

After his Midwestern conference and a trip onward to San Francisco to speak at a college, Andy returned to Harford Place resolved to accept the loss of his hand and to make lasting peace with Flora. Andy will strive for all he is worth to set an example for his community of how to remain a marginal farmer while the industrial farmers of America continue their agrarian trajectory downward.

THE IMAGE OF JUDGMENT

The biblical image of judgment casts light on virtually the whole of Berry's work. He speaks with a voice of prophecy about the future of America. Part of this prophecy is pessimistic; part is optimistic.

Berry's pessimism is suggested by the mere title of one collection of his essays, *Another Turn of the Crank*. Committed readers of Berry have become so familiar with his themes and causes that they can anticipate what he will say before he says it. But this is not to suggest that what he says is not worth hearing in any new venue he presents it. Agrarian and environmental messages bear repetition in a society that is too willing to forget them.

In an essay titled "The Agrarian Standard," Berry indicates that as an agrarian writer he sees himself in the position of an underdog. Despite his efforts and those of thousands of less public figures across America who speak out for nature, the juggernaut of what we mistakenly call "progress" rolls on: displacement of rural people; strip mining; mitigation of wetlands; encroachment on wilderness; urban sprawl; gentrification of countryside; government construction projects; and commercial and industrial development. The slogan that appears on the American dollar bill "In God we trust" might aptly be changed to "Nothing is enough." In the face of all this, Berry says, "One keeps writing essays and speeches that one would prefer not to write, that one wishes would prove unnecessary, that one hopes nobody will have any need for in twenty-five years."[20] But in his pessimism he has little confidence that such essays and speeches will not be needed in the future, for he doubts that American society will curb exploitation of its natural resources.

The optimistic part of Berry's prophecy for the future of America is a hope for a Great Awakening. Such awakenings occurred in American society during the eighteenth and nineteenth centuries when people took extra caution about the salvation of their souls. Berry implicitly calls for such awakening, this time taking extra caution about the salvation of nature as necessary to the salvation of souls.

Berry's fellow agrarian Gene Logsdon published a small book titled *The Man Who Created Paradise: A Fable*,[21] for which Berry wrote the Foreword. It tells the story of Wally Spero who left his job as a metal grinder in a foundry to take on the challenge of transforming one of the most devastated areas of America, the strip-mined spoil banks of south-eastern Ohio. Wally bought land cheaply and went to work on it with an ancient bulldozer. Year by year he scraped and fashioned hundreds of acres of raw subsoil to create fields, pastures ponds, and gentle hills. He planted trees, made gardens, and sowed grasses till he had turned an area of environmental disaster into a place called Paradise Farm. People of the region captured Wally's vision. They spruced up their farms and communities, established cottage industries, and began to get along with one another as though human nature had been reborn. It is a fable, a utopian vision, but without a vision we cannot see where it might be good to go. In Berry's work, that is what the biblical vision of Paradise is for, to give direction. It is obviously not a direction shared by everyone in American society today. But little by little, agrarians and environmentalists, by writing essays, making speeches, and tending their own gardens, just might make a beneficent difference in the America of tomorrow.

Berry's optimism is sustained by an underlying religious faith, which he expresses in a sentence of *The Unsettling of America*: "For our healing we have on our side one great force: the power of Creation, with good care, with kindly use, to heal itself."[22] The blending of pessimism and optimism in Berry's work recalls the biblical prophet Jeremiah, the weeping prophet of hope.

Notes

1. Wendell Berry, "Christianity and the Survival of Creation," *Sex, Economy, and Community* (New York: Pantheon Books, 1993), 93-116.

2. Wendell Berry, *A Timbered Choir: The Sabbath Poems* 1979-1997 (Washington D.C.: Counterpoint, 1998), 40.

3. Wendell Berry, "The Gift of Good Land," *The Gift of Good Land* (New York: North Point Press, Farrar, Straus and Giroux, 1981), 275.

4. Wendell Berry, "Conservation and Local Economy," *Sex, Economy and Community*, 11.

5. Wendell Berry, *Harlan Hubbard: Life and Work* (New York: Pantheon Books, 1990), 86.

6. Berry, *Harlan Hubbard*, 87.

7. Berry, *Harlan Hubbard*, 86.

8. Berry, "Christianity and the Survival of Creation," *Sex, Economy and Community*, 97.

9. Wendell Berry, *The Memory of Old Jack* (Washington, D.C.: Counterpoint, 1999), 39.

10. Berry, *The Memory of Old Jack*, 60.

11. Leo Tolstoy, "How Much Land Does a Man Need?" *The Kreutzer Sonata and Other Short Stories* (New York: Dover Publications, 1993).

12. Berry, *The Memory of Old Jack*, 169.

13. Berry, *The Memory of Old Jack*, 170.

14. *Wendell Berry, The Unsettling of America: Culture and Agriculture* (San Francisco: Sierra Club Books, 1986), 59.

15. Wendell Berry, *Remembering* (San Francisco: North Point Press, 1988), 10.

16. Berry, *Remembering*, 19.

17. Berry, *Remembering*, 60.

18. Berry, *Remembering*, 61.
19. Berry, *Remembering*, 66.
20. Wendell Berry, "The Agrarian Standard," *Citizenship Papers* (Washington DC: Shoemaker and Hoard, 2003), 143.
21. Gene Logsdon, *The Man Who Created Paradise: A Fable* (Athens: Ohio University Press, 1998).
22. Berry, *The Unsettling of America*, 223.

7

LOUIS BROMFIELD'S DREAM OF LIFE AT MALABAR FARM

Where there is no vision, the people perish.

—PROVERBS 29:18

I N THE SECOND quarter of the twentieth century, the Ohio writer Louis Bromfield was one of the best-known literary figures in the United States. During his literary career, he published twenty-four books of fiction and seven books of nonfiction. Bromfield is best remembered for the books that deal with his dream of achieving a self-sufficient life in an environment of rural nature.

Bromfield's life story is rich and varied. He was born in Mansfield, Ohio in 1896. In growing up, he was intimate with the woods and farmlands of the surrounding countryside. His maternal grandfather was a farmer, and Bromfield's father, though forced by economic circumstances to find jobs in the city, was always a farmer at heart.

Bromfield wanted to become a farmer, but his mother had other aspirations for him. She wanted him to become a writer. Upon graduating from public school, he went to Cornell agricultural college, but remained only a few months before returning to Ohio to work on a farm. It was hard work without financial promise. It dawned on him that his mother's aspirations for his life were sound. He enrolled at Columbia to study journalism, where again he remained only a few months. The First World War was in progress, and now, on the cusp of manhood, he volunteered for the American Army to serve as an ambulance driver and interpreter in France. For his participation in several battles, the French government awarded him the *Croix de Guerre* for extraordinary bravery.

At the end of the war, Bromfield returned to the United States and found journalistic work in New York City. Not only did he have a gift for writing, but also for socializing. He met and married in 1921 the daughter of a wealthy New England family, Mary Appleton Wood, who bore the couple's first daughter in 1924. In that same year, the young journalist had financial success with the publication of *The Green Bay Tree*, the first in a series of four novels—including *Possession* (1925), *Early Autumn* (1926), and *A Good Woman* (1927)— dealing with social manners and values in American society.

As a soldier, Bromfield had loved France, its culture, and people. During a vacation trip back to France in 1925, he and his wife decided to take up residence in Senlis, a town thirty-five miles northeast of Paris. They took a fifty-year lease on an old stone house called the Presbytère, which sat on acreage that had once been a Capuchin monastery. For thirteen years the Bromfields lived in Senlis, where their family expanded with the birth of two more daughters. During those years, the Presbytère became a meeting place for notable Americans and Europeans who came to partake of the Bromfields' celebrated Sunday lunches. Among their friends during the Senlis years were the American expatriates Gertrude Stein and Edith Wharton.

As a novelist, Bromfield's literary reputation grew, and for his third novel, *Early Autumn*, he won the Pulitzer Prize in 1927. He traveled to India and throughout Europe and gathered materials for future novels. Hollywood sought him out as a writer of movie scripts, for which he earned considerable money. But for all of his literary and financial success, the boyhood dream to become a farmer never left him. Throughout his years in France he kept a sizeable garden on the grounds of the former monastery. He later regarded as one of his greatest honors of his life a diploma he received from the French government for his gardening efforts on French soil.

Under the gathering clouds of the Second World War, Bromfield in 1938 returned to the United States with his family. With money in his pocket, and the promise as an established literary figure of earning more, he bought three worn-out farms in a valley situated a few miles southeast of his native city of Mansfield, Ohio. He combined the three farms into one, and named it Malabar after a beautiful place he had visited in India. At Malabar, he began to realize his dream of creating a self-sufficient farm where he and his family could live in bucolic contentment.

Bromfield hired an agricultural expert and several farm workers to help him restore the worn-out land. With the aid of an architect and a bevy of carpenters, he renovated an old farmhouse into a thirty-two-room country manor, where over the years he regularly entertained guests. He continued to write fiction, and movie scripts, but increasingly wrote books and articles on rural life, agriculture, and agricultural economics. Public recognition of these writings outstripped that of his fiction, and the Malabar he had created became famous throughout the United States.

I would like to be able to conclude this biographical sketch of Louis Bromfield with the words, "And he lived happily ever after." But truth would not be served by those words. The truth is, his life at Malabar was a seventeen-year struggle to realize a dream that met with considerable disillusionment. At the time of his death of bone cancer in 1956, at age fifty-nine, his reputation as a fiction writer had long been in decline. His wife Mary had preceded him in death, as had George Hawkins, his trusted companion and business manager of many years. He was at odds with his children, and so pressed with debt that he sold off the timber rights on Malabar to pay his hospital bills. His last hope was that somehow Malabar would survive him.

After Bromfield's death, an old friend, the tobacco heiress Doris Duke, stepped in and bought back the timber rights and returned them to the estate. Malabar did survive much as Bromfield left it, and today is an Ohio State Park that thousands of people visit each year. Tour guides of the "Big House" display the bedroom where Humphrey Bogart and Lauren Bacall spent their wedding night; point out the claw and teeth marks that Bromfield's Boxer dogs made on doors and furniture; and highlight the magnificent rounded desk that Bromfield designed. Somehow, the desk seems symbolic of Malabar as a whole. Though Bromfield was physically a big man, the desk turned out to be of too great a height for him to sit at comfortably while writing. He wrote while seated at a card table.

In the Introduction to The Wooster Book Company's reissue of Bromfield's *Pleasant Valley*, Ohio farmer and writer Gene Logsdon notes that Bromfield came "close to being two totally different people: . . . Bromfield, the careful planter of crops in rotation, and Bromfield the profligate sower of wild oats in exhilaration."[1] Bromfield succumbed to the temptation to become an entertainer outside his writing. "He became a showman," says Logsdon, "and his farm a showplace."[2]

I have visited Malabar many times. In connection with those visits I have often thought of Marie Antoinette's make-believe country village at Versailles, where she and others in amateur theatrical performances played the roles of shepherds and shepherdesses. Malabar was also a place of make-believe. Bromfield had a house rule that if his guests were to eat they either had to work or stay out of the way. Often his guests were movie stars who were accustomed to the world of make believe. Rather than stay out of the way, some played the role of farmer. Joan Fontaine oversaw the birth of a calf; Kay Francis stirred apple butter with a wooden hoe.[3]

Showman though he was, Bromfield made significant practical contributions to modern farming. He was among the first to suspect the widespread dangers of the use of DDT as a pesticide, even before Rachel Carson's exposé of those dangers in her book *Silent Spring*. And he demonstrated that it was possible to bring worn-out and eroded farm land back to a state of productive health through heavy composting, grass production, rotation and contour planting, and what is today recognized as no-till farming.

More prominent in my view than the practical contributions Bromfield made to modern farming is the personal understanding of life he gave expression to in the creation of Malabar. That understanding of life—which I call his "dream of Malabar"—involves three major themes: of being *"teched,"* of the *rightness* of nature, and of *care* for the earth and all its creatures.

THE THEME OF BEING "TECHED"

In his novel *The Farm*, Bromfield renders a broad picture of the history of farming in Ohio from the time of the pioneers to the end of the nineteenth century when rural life was steadily giving way to city life and industrialism. A main character in the novel is a businessman and politician modeled on Bromfield's father, whose habit of buying and restoring worn-out farms kept his family in financial quicksand. Financially imprudent though the father was, he passed on to his children his love of the land and the things of nature. "What he gave them," Bromfield writes, "was destined to stay with them forever. It was the most precious heritage one could receive. He was a man who knew how to live. He knew the things that count."[4]

In a collection of his short stories titled *The World We Live In*, Bromfield included "Up Ferguson Way," a narrative that pays tribute to his father and underscores "things that count" in his own understanding of life. In the story, he remembers an eventful day when he was about eight years old. It was election time and his father was running for office. The father took the boy with him in a horse-drawn buggy on a campaign trip throughout the countryside. At one farm they visited, the father declined an invitation to stay for dinner because he wanted to get "up Ferguson way" before noon. The father and the boy descended into a beautiful rolling valley, then travelled a rocky road through a dense woods. The road led to the top of the highest hill of the landscape where sat the Ferguson farm. In the weathered farmhouse lived Zenobia Ferguson, a woman some sixty years old who had lived on the farm since the death of her parents years back.

Zenobia's life was marked by a tragic incident. When she was a young woman, she killed her lover with a shotgun blast through a door of the farmhouse, mistaking him for robbers who had been menacing the countryside. She was exonerated of the killing, but steadily grew reclusive and eccentric in her ways. Some people said she was "teched," but the father knew her for a wise woman.

Zenobia was a "handsome, fierce creature," Bromfield writes, with the figure of a boy, black hair, and riveting black eyes that betrayed her Delaware Indian heritage. Upon his meeting her for the first time, Zenobia took the boy's face in her hands and studied it intently, then announced to the father, "Yes. He'll do. He has the right kind of eye…You know, you can tell people and animals by their eyes."[5]

While Zenobia prepared a meal and talked with the father, the boy wandered Zenobia's property. "In that jungle of old lilacs and rose bushes," Bromfield remembers,

> the birds came very close. A robin sat on a lilac bough not three feet from me and watched while I ate the grapes. A squirrel sat without fear on the eaves of the old log house and chattered and made faces at me. And the sight of all these things made the heart of that small boy sing, I think because all these living things seemed so near and so without strangeness or fear. It was as if this little world existing high against the blue October sky were a small paradise, a little world that was what all the great world should be.[6]

Zenobia interrupted the boy's adventure outside with a call to dinner. At the meal, the boy quietly observed to the father that there was no meat served. "You mustn't speak about that," the father cautioned. "Zenobia never kills anything."[7] After the meal, the father took a nap, while the boy again went outside and found his way to the pond below the spring house. "I began digging in the mud," Bromfield says,

> while the ducks swam in close to watch me, turning their heads on one side in duck fashion to satisfy their curiosity. They chattered a great deal among themselves. The cow came down to the pond to drink, the new calf teetering on its long legs, moving forward in jerky sudden movements. I stopped digging to watch and suddenly the calf became my brother, a small creature for whom I felt a sudden intense love, quite different from the sort of love I felt for any person, even my own parents or my brothers or sisters. It was as if we were both a part of something which other people did not understand, a whole world apart in which there were sounds which no human could understand. I knew suddenly what the ducks were quacking about and understood the look in the great brown eyes of the Jersey cow. The squirrel came down to the edge of the pond and did a curious thing. He dipped both his tiny paws into the water and then put them into his mouth and cleaned them with his tiny pink tongue.[8]

Sensing that someone was watching him, the boy turned to discover Zenobia standing near the springhouse. She had changed from the man's clothing she had been wearing earlier to an old-fashioned purple dress. "She was smiling at me," Bromfield says, "and suddenly I had for her the same feeling of fathomless understanding I had experienced for the ducks, the cow, and the squirrels." Zenobia in a soft voice beckoned a squirrel to come to her. "The squirrel made a chattering noise," and Zenobia said to the boy, "He's asking who you are and what your're doing here." Then she said to the squirrel, "It's all right. He knows what we know. He may forget it someday but in the end, it will come back to him. He's one of those that is teched like us."[9]

Zenobia died old and feeble. Bromfield had often thought about his boyhood experience of meeting her. One day he saddled a horse to ride from Malabar up the road through the woods to the Ferguson farm, taking his Boxer dogs with him. The farmhouse was gone but the springhouse was still there. After drinking from the spring, he lay back to rest. Bromfield recalls those moments:

> It was not only good to be alive, it was good to be alive in this particular spot on the surface of the earth. And slowly I began to feel again that sensation I had known as a small boy, of coming up out of the valley into another strange world that somehow existed on a different plane from all other human life. . . . It was almost as if I could understand what the birds were saying as they chirped and sang in the ruins of the old garden.
>
> Then suddenly I felt that I was being watched by someone or something, exactly as I had felt on that October day as a small boy when Zenobia appeared suddenly among the bushes beside the spring house in the purple dress. I turned and found myself saying "Zenobia." It was the strangest sensation I have ever experienced, of reaching into another world, of being almost at the brink of understanding.[10]

When he was leaving the Ferguson Farm to ride back down into the valley, he saw a woodchuck that showed no fear of him or the Boxer dogs. He playfully urged the dogs to chase the woodchuck, never thinking that they would catch it. But they caught and killed it. Bromfield felt sick. "I had done an awful thing," he laments, "I had betrayed Zenobia and the squirrel. I had violated all that world of which I had been permitted to be a part . . . a world into which I could enter because I was "teched." . . . I had done a dreadful thing. . . . I never again took the dogs when I went "up Ferguson way."[11]

At the conclusion of the story, Bromfield describes a journal Zenobia had kept that came into his possession by chance:

> The Journal took a little reading and a great deal of understanding, but after a while it became clear. The names Zenobia used were not the names of people but of animals. The conversations were not conversations with people but with the birds and the beasts of the fields and the forests. . . . Zenobia had lived in a world peopled by friends which none of the others of us could ever know or understand, unless you were, like Zenobia and the squirrel, a little "teched."[12]

Bromfield said that he drew insight and inspiration from a teaching of the Jains of India who held that "the principle of life itself, even in an insect, is sacred and of God." The significance of that teaching, he divulges, has "welled up in me many times in contact with animals and trees and landscape, at moments when I was certain not only of the existence of God but of my own immortality as part of some gigantic scheme of creation."[13] Bromfield used the word "teched" to describe persons, like Zenobia, who had an intuitive grasp of the principle of life itself. He also meant by the word that such persons were blessed.

THE THEME OF THE RIGHTNESS OF NATURE

The second major theme of Bromfield's dream of Malabar is the *rightness* of nature. He insisted that whether a person were making a garden, building a house, or designing a farm, the person should attempt to observe a *"rightness* in relation to the whole landscape, to the climate, to the country, to the regional architecture, to the type of soils, . .to the existence of the natural birds and wildlife. It should have a relation to the past of the region, to history itself."[14]

In building the "Big House" at Malabar, Bromfield wanted it to blend in with the natural features of the landscape. He writes:

> I wanted a house which after a year or two looked as if it belonged there on that hillside shelf in the middle of the rich Ohio country, a house that looked as if it had been there since the clearing of the wilderness, above all, a big house which would not stick up like a sore thumb in the midst of a beautiful landscape.[15]

Perhaps Bromfield never heard of the ancient Chinese philosophy of nature called *feng shui*, which has become familiar to Westerners in recent years, but he would probably have been sympathetic toward that philosophy. *Feng shui* teaches that forces in nature such as wind and water achieve a certain rightness in nature that humans can feel but not see, grasp but not hold. The challenge to humans—if they seek to live in harmony with nature—is to feel and grasp the rightness nature has achieved in relation to a given environment, and to adapt their living habits to that rightness.

In his book *Pleasant Valley,* Bromfield devotes a chapter titled "My Ninety Acres" to Walter Oakes, a person whom he regarded as having felt and grasped nature's rightness in relation to the place where he lived. Walter Oakes owned a ninety-acre farm in the vicinity of Malabar. When in his twenties, he had married the prettiest and most intelligent girl in the county. Nobody could understand why Nellie Oakes chose Walter over "Homer Drake, whose father owned four hundred and fifty acres of the best land in the country or Jim Neilson, whose family owned the bank and feed mill in Darlington."[16] Time proved that Nellie had made the right choice. After Homer inherited his father's farm, it gradually went to ruin, and Jim Neilson after losing the bank and mill died a drunkard. All Walter had was ninety acres of poor hill land that he "bought because he didn't have money enough for anything better."[17] But it was enough for Nellie. She loved Walter, and understood that he was a man who would make the best of what he had.

Nellie died with the birth of their second son. Walter never remarried. A widow woman came to keep house and to look after him and the boys. People talked about possible intimacy between Walter and the widow, but there was nothing to it. And, besides, Walter was not one to worry much about what people thought or said. He focused on rearing his boys and farming his ninety acres.

Nellie had been a shrewd observer of nature. She used to say to Walter that "a farm could teach you more than you could teach it, if you just kept your eyes open."[18] She had wanted the farm to appear as though it belonged to the landscape, and that's the way Walter had kept it over all the years since her death.

Walter's elder son, John, died in the First World War. His younger son, Robert, moved away from home and became president of a metals corporation and a millionaire. Walter lived on the farm alone. On Sundays Bromfield would drive over from Malabar to visit with him. There was a certain "romantic shagginess" about Walter's ninety acres that Bromfield greatly admired. In describing the natural features surrounding the house, Bromfield writes:

> The . . . shagginess appeared . . . in the garden around the small white house with its green shutters that stood beneath two ancient Norway spruces. The patches of lawn were kept neatly

— 90 —

mowed but surrounding them grew a jungle of old-fashioned flowers and shrubs—lilacs, standing honeysuckle, syringe, bleeding heart, iris, peonies, tiger lilies, day lilies, old-fashioned roses like the Seven Sisters and the piebald and the Baltimore Belle. At the back the little vegetable garden was neat enough with its rows of vegetables and its peach and pear and quince trees in a row inside the white picket fence. But beyond the borders of the garden, the shagginess continued. There weren't any bright, new, clean wire fences. The wire along the fence rows was hidden beneath sassafras and elderberry and wild black raspberry and the wood lot on the hill above the creek was not a clean place with the grass eaten short by cattle. The cattle had been fenced out and the trees, from seedlings to great oaks grew rankly with a tropical luxuriance.[19]

During those Sunday visits, Bromfield and Walter would walk the fields and fence rows of Walter's ninety acres. "We would make a round of the small empire," Bromfield recalls, "while old Walter told me the history of each field and what had happened to it, what he had learned from this field or that one." It was as though Walter were trying to feel and grasp what nature had to teach him what it would permit and reward in terms of his efforts to foster its productivity. As a result, Bromfield insists, Walter's "alfalfa and clover were thicker than those of his neighbors, his corn higher and sturdier, his Herefords bigger and fatter."[20]

During one Sunday visit, they discovered a nest of quails in a fence row. "They used to laugh at me, Walter said, "for letting the bushes grow up in my fence rows, but they don't any more. When the chinch bugs come along all ready to eat up my corn, these little fellows will take care of 'em. . . . There's nothing a quail likes as much as a chinch bug."[21]

Walter, as Bromfield's ideal farmer, took account of everything that was happening on his ninety acres, to produce, as Bromfield describes it, "the most beautiful farm in America. . . . The rich fields were like one of the opulent women painted by Rubens, like a woman well-loved whose beauty thrives and increases by love-makng."[22]

The narrative continues with Bromfield's account of a visit he received from Walter's son, Robert. One October day a "big, shiny black car" came up the lane to Malabar. Bromfield walked out to greet his visitor. "He was plump and rather flabby with pouches beneath the eyes which looked through the shining lenses of steel-rimmed spectacles. He stooped a little and there was a certain softness about his chin and throat."[23] After lunch, Robert approached Bromfield with the purpose of his visit. He wanted Bromfield to persuade Walter to leave his ninety acres for "a fruit ranch in Florida or Southern California, or a bigger farm, or a flat in New York."[24] Bromfield was touched by Robert's concern for his father's welfare, but also amused. He writes:

We were both silent for a time and then I said, "Honestly, Bob, I don't think there's anything to be done and to tell the truth I don't see why we should do anything. He's as happy as it's possible for a man to be. He's tough as nails and he loves that place like a woman." Then hesitantly, I said, "Besides, Nellie is always there looking after him."

A startled look came into the son's blue eyes and after a moment he asked, "Do you feel that way, too?"

I said, "I think Nellie is everywhere in that ninety acres. He's never lonely. She's in the garden and the fields and his famous fence rows. She's out there husking corn with him now in the bottom forty."[25]

A few weeks later, Bromfield went over to Walter's for his Sunday visit to find the old man dead in his bed. He notified Robert. After the funeral, Robert decided not to sell Walter's farm. Bromfield undertook to farm it for Robert, and sent one of his hired workers to live in Walter's house. "But it will never be farmed," Bromfield concludes, "as old Walter farmed it. There isn't anybody who will ever farm that earth again as if it were the only woman he ever loved."[26]

The chapter "My Ninety Acres" is writing that illuminates Bromfield's passionate love for the earth and his deep intuitions about the rightness of nature. To live in an environment is not simply to be there, but to be there as nature would have us be part of it. The rightness of human activity in a given environment is determined by the greater rightness of nature in its shaping of that environment over centuries of ripening activity.

THE THEME OF CARE FOR THE EARTH AND ALL ITS CREATURES

In the prime of his career at Malabar, Bromfield had a portrait painted of himself. In it he is posed not with his wife or children, but with one of his Boxer dogs. They are seated on a large rock with the barn at Malabar in the background. Bromfield has an arm around the dog. As they appear in profile looking off to the left, there is a striking similarity between the head of the dog and the head of the man. Bromfield had a profound empathy not just with dogs, but with animals in general. One of his finest gifts as a writer was his ability to observe and describe animal life. This gift is exemplified in a chapter titled "A Hymn to Hawgs," contained in his book *From My Experience*.

To many people a pig is basically something to be eaten in the form of bacon. But for Bromfield, the pig was a highly intelligent creature deserving of utmost respect. He says:

If I have ever doubted a pig's capacity to think things out, I lost it forever when I discovered one pig's trick of escaping through what was by every reasonable evidence a thoroughly pig-tight fence . . . . Late one afternoon as I stood in the far end of the field . . . I saw what I found difficult to believe. At the opposite end of the field I saw a pig actually *climbing* the fence.[27]

The bemused Bromfield kept regular watch on the pig over the coming weeks. It had learned that the cornfield across the road contained food that was more to its liking than what it found in the hog lot. The pig eventually ate itself out of freedom, for each day it grew larger in girth. The day came when "he was unable to find an opening to permit his escape or to reach the top of the fence without falling backward into the prison of his hog lot."[28] That pig, Bromfield maintains, possessed "great powers of logic, reflection, judgment, deduction, and mockery, qualities which man has usually and often mistakenly reserved for himself"[29]

Bromfield collected his writings about animal life in a late book *Animals and Other People.* In an Introductory Note, he writes:

In the last analysis we are all animals and the fact of being born a man does not endow us with any special rights or virtues; rather it imposes upon us obligations of a high sort indeed, which animals and birds do not share—obligations of intelligence, ethics, decency, loyalty and moral behavior. The sad thing is how frequently these obligations are violated and ignored by man himself.[30]

In this passage, Bromfield strikes an ethical chord that became increasingly pronounced in his last years. He was pondering the question of humanity's ethical responsibility toward the animal kingdom and toward nature as a whole. In conjunction with this question he was trying to comprehend why at Malabar he "had poured out time and energy and money in very large amounts for things on which there could not possibly be any material return."[31]

While reading Albert Schweitzer's autobiography *Out of My Life and Thought*, Bromfield came upon the phrase "Reverence for Life." This phrase, as he explains in his book *From My Experience*, provided a shock of personal recognition. "I began to understand what it was that had taken increasing possession of me for fifteen years, indeed, for nearly a generation; why I had committed what some of my fellow men regarded as follies, but which were not follies at all." He also read in Schweitzer the following sentence, "'A man is ethical only when life, as such, is sacred to him, that of plants and animals as well as that of his fellow men, and when he devotes himself helpfully to all life that is in need of help.'"[32] Bromfield came to recognize that all along, in his struggle to create Malabar, in his desire to work with nature rather than against it, in his writing about plants, animals, and people, he had moved toward a Reverence for Life. "This principle," he goes on to say,

> is known to every *good* farmer, as it is known to every truly good and truly happy person. It is unfortunate that we are sometimes weak enough to sin against it, and each time we sin we suffer a weakening of our dignity. The sin can be committed in countless ways, from unkindness to the greedy ravaging of a forest, from the making of a "smart deal" to the wasting of land which belongs not to us but to Life, and which we hold only in trust for future generations.[33]

"Sin" is properly a religious term. Within the disciplines of philosophy, sociology, psychology and environmentalism, it is rarely used.

Bromfield did use it because he found no other term that quite captured the sense of humanity's disregard for its responsibility of care for the earth and all its creatures. In the twilight of his career, Bromfield said, "I am a very religious man and somewhat of a mystic."[34] I doubt he could have found truer words to describe himself.

THE RELEVANCE OF BROMFIELD'S DREAM OF LIFE AT MALABAR FOR ENVIRONMENTAL THOUGHT TODAY

In the writings of Bromfield I have discussed, sentimentality is a factor. Sentimentality is essentially a screen of feeling that we put between ourselves and life. Our feelings take priority over the actual life we observe. Anybody who has been associated with farm life knows it is filled with sweat, stench, flies and backbreaking work. There is a marked difference between Thomas Hardy's or Willa Cather's non-sentimental accounts—which bring us up against the harshness of farm life—and Bromfield's sentimental accounts.

If we are greatly put off by Bromfield's sentimentality, we do not have to indulge in it by reading him. But if we do read him—sentimentality and all—we have in focus an important aspect of the American Dream: the Jeffersonian ideal of the happy, independent yeoman who finds sanctuary from the multiple problems of society amid the simple pleasures of nature. This is not the get-rich aspect of the American Dream, but the find-happiness aspect of it.

There was no greater booster of the Jeffersonian aspect of the American Dream in the first half of twentieth century than Bromfield. It lingers in the ambitions of persons who seek a life in the countryside where they can escape congested traffic, have a few acres, keep a garden, raise animals, and rear children free of undesired external influences. In many parts of America, rural countryside is becoming increasingly hard to find and costly to buy. As America in the twenty-first century becomes steadily more populated—perhaps doubling by the end of the twenty-first century—competition for space, privacy, and simple pleasures of nature will grow more intense. We may no longer be able to move outward to the rural countryside in pursuit of the Jeffersonian aspect of the American Dream.

In his book *Staying Put: Making a Home in a Restless World*, Scott Russell Sanders has given a good deal of thought to the Jeffersonian aspect of the American Dream that I am considering. Sanders contends that we do not have to move outward to pursue the American Dream. We can pursue it in places where we find ourselves, in our homes, backyard gardens, and places where we work. The places we inhabit should be "intimately known, worked on, dreamed over, cherished."[35] In contrast to a way of life that involves "pulling up stakes and heading for new territory," Sanders advocates a way of life that involves "standing your ground, confronting the powers, going deeper."[36]

Sanders' phrase "going deeper" is appropriate for characterizing Bromfield's dream of life at Malabar. It is a dream about going deeper, about being touched by the mysteries of nature; about trying to feel and grasp the rightness of nature in our environment; about having empathy with and ethical concern for forms of life that are different from our own. Most of all, it is a dream about having Reverence for Life.

In reading Bromfield—especially his story "Up Ferguson Way"—I am reminded that in Greek mythology gods and goddesses have interchanges with mortals. The myth of Artemis and Actaeon comes to mind. Artemis was goddess of wild things, animals, places, fertility, and motherly care. Down through time she was identified by other names. The Romans in their mythology identified her as the goddess Diana. Artemis was a protective goddess but also a strict one. She punished mortals who failed to show reverence toward her.

Actaeon, a hunter, offended her by daring to gaze upon her naked-
ness while she was bathing in her sacred spring. Artemis turned him
into a stag, and his own hounds devoured him. Bromfield as a farmer
and writer about "things that count"[37] showed reverence toward her.
She was not offended that he called her "Zenobia."

NOTES

1. Gene Logsdon, "Introduction," *Pleasant Valley* (Wooster, Ohio: The Wooster Book Company, 1997), xi.
2. Logsdon, "Introduction," *Pleasant Valley*, xii.
3. Ellen Bromfield Geld, *The Heritage: A Daughter's Memories of Louis Bromfield.* (Athens, Ohio: Ohio University Press, 1999), 106.
4. Louis Bromfield, *The Farm* (N.Y: Aeonian Press, 1976), 277.
5. Louis Bromfield, "Up Ferguson Way," *The World We Live In: Stories by Louis Bromfield* (Philadelphia: The Blakiston Company, 1944), 245.
6. Bromfield, "Up Ferguson Way," 246.
7. Bromfield "Up Ferguson Way," 248.
8. Bromfield "Up Ferguson Way," 248-49.
9. Bromfield, "Up Ferguson Way," 249.
10. Bromfield "Up Ferguson Way," 265.
11. Bromfield, "Up Ferguson Way," 268.
12. Bromfield, "Up Ferguson Way," 269.
13. Louis Bromfield, *Pleasant Valley* (Wooster, Ohio: The Wooster Book Company, 1997), 293.
14. Louis Bromfield, *From My Experience* (Wooster, Ohio: The Wooster Book Company, 1999), 72.
15. Bromfield, *Pleasant Valley*, 76.
16. Bromfield, *Pleasant Valley*, 137.
17. Bromfield, *Pleasant Valley*, 137.
18. Bromfield, *Pleasant Valley*, 145.
19. Bromfield, *Pleasant Valley*, 136-37.
20. Bromfield, *Pleasant Valley*, 149.
21. Bromfield, *Pleasant Valley*, 145.
22. Bromfield, *Pleasant Valley*, 142.
23. Bromfield, *Pleasant Valley*, 150.
24. Bromfield, *Pleasant Valley*, 151.

25. Bromfield, *Pleasant Valley*, 152.
26. Bromfield, *Pleasant Valley*, 155.
27. Bromfield, *From My Experience*, 17.
28. Bromfield, *From My Experience*, 18.
29. Bromfield, *From My Experience*, 17.
30. Louis Bromfield, *Animals and Other People* (New York: Harper and Brothers, 1955), xii.
31. Bromfield, *From My Experience*, 304.
32. Bromfield, *From My Experience*, 304.
33. Bromfield, *From My Experience*, 305.
34. Bromfield, *From My Experience*, 299.
35. Scott Russell Sanders, *Staying Put: Making a Home in a Restless World* (Boston: Beacon Press, 1993), 101.
36. Sanders, *Staying Put*, 102.
37. *Bromfield, The Farm*, 277.

8

SHAKESPEARE'S IMAGINARY GARDENS AND THE TEACHING OF LIFE

Il faut cultiver notre jardin—We must cultivate our garden.

—VOLTAIRE, *CANDIDE*

M Y TEACHER OF Shakespeare when I was in college was a frail, aging lady who did not hold a PhD, but who knew English literature, and especially her Shakespeare. "Miss Weaver," as students formally addressed her, opened the first day of class with the remark, "What you are going to get in this course in Shakespeare is a little piece of me." At the time I thought her remark strange, if not silly. I wanted to learn objectively the plots and characters of Shakespeare's plays, to investigate the scholarship that surrounded them. Over the years, I have many times recalled Miss Weaver's remark. She held to an affective or personal approach to Shakespeare. When she read her favorite passages aloud, the words glowed on her face. She made features of Shakespeare her own, and encouraged students to do the same.

A feature of Shakespeare I have made my own is a fascination with gardens. By 1597 he had earned enough money from his work as a playwright of the London stage that he was able to buy New House back in his home village of Stratford-upon-Avon. New House stood on extensive grounds. To the rear of the house were barns and elm trees. His property deeds mention two gardens and two orchards. If you visit the site of New House today, a tour guide may point out in the "great Garden" an aged mulberry tree grown as a start from a tree that Shakespeare himself planted. The story, as with many surrounding Shakespeare's life, must be taken with a grain of salt. It is certain, however, that he created imaginary gardens in his plays.

The concept of a garden implies human presence and activity. A garden is a plot of earth designated for the cultivation of flowers, vegetables, herbs, fruit, and sometimes designated primarily for aesthetic pleasure. Humans put a great deal of themselves into their gardens. The garden a person keeps hints at the character of its keeper. Is it large or small, practical or ornamental, weeded or not weeded? When Shakespeare creates an imaginary garden, the imagery tells something about the person or persons whom he associates with the garden. I am focused here on the imaginary gardens he creates in relation to the characters of Friar Lawrence in *Romeo and Juliet*, Ophelia in *Hamlet*, Richard the Second in *Richard the Second,* and Lorenzo and Jessica in *The Merchant of Venice*.[1]

THE GARDEN OF FRIAR LAWRENCE

When Friar Lawrence first appears in *Romeo and Juliet* he is alone, carrying a willow basket for gathering plants from the monastery garden. He speaks in soliloquy:

> The grey-ey'd morn smiles on the frowning night,
> Chek'ring the eastern clouds with streaks of light,
> And fleckled darkness like a drunkard reels
> From forth day's path and Titan's [fiery] wheels.
> Now ere the sun advance his burning eye,
> The day to cheer and night's dank dew to dry,
> I must up-fill this osier cage of ours
> With baleful weeds and precious-juiced flowers.
> The earth that's nature's mother is her tomb;
> What is her burying grave, that is her womb;
> And from her womb children of divers kind
> We sucking on her natural bosom find:
> Many for many virtues excellent,
> None but for some, and yet all different.
> O, mickle is the powerful grace that lies
> In plants, herbs, stones, and their true qualities;
> For nought so vile that on earth doth live
> But to the earth some special good doth give;
> Nor aught so good but, strain'd from that fair use,
> Revolts from true birth, stumbling on abuse.

Virtue itself turns vice, being misapplied,
And vice sometime by action dignified.

(II. iii. 1-23)

Shakespeare conveys several thoughts in these lines. The Friar gathers weeds in his basket along with flowers and herbs. He is practical in his work, weeding and harvesting at the same time. The Friar is a philosophical naturalist. He reflects on the "powerful grace" that fills the earth with "children of divers kind," "baleful weeds" as well as "precious-juiced flowers." Is anything in nature corrupt in itself? Even weeds have a place in nature's scheme. The words "virtue" and "vice" in the soliloquy have a moral valence. Humans are challenged to be vigilant gardeners amid the virtues and vices of life.

In the course of the play, the Friar proves to be less than a vigilant gardener of the virtues and vices. Initially he is hesitant to perform the marriage of Romeo and Juliet, but then changes his mind. If he marries them secretly, the marriage might bring about reconciliation between the warring families of the Montagues and Capulets. There is an old saying, "O what a tangled web we weave when we practice to deceive." Things do not go as the Friar plans.

After Romeo kills Tybalt, he escapes to Mantua. Juliet's parents do not know that she is married to Romeo, and insist that she marry Paris. In despair, Juliet consults the Friar, who advises her to deceive her parents by seeming to agree to the marriage with Paris. He gives her a sleeping potion that for a time will cause her to appear as dead. Instead of being married to Paris, she will be carried to the Capulet's burial vault in the churchyard, and by the time she wakes, Romeo will have had the opportunity to return and take her away to Mantua.

The Friar sends a letter to Romeo in Mantua to tell him of the scheme, but it does not reach him. Romeo hears of Juliet's death, and buys poison from an apothecary in Mantua with the intention of returning to Verona and joining Juliet in death. When he is prying open her vault, Paris appears on the scene. He and Romeo argue, and Paris is mortally wounded in a duel. After an exchange of conciliatory words between the two. Romeo poisons himself and dies.

When the Friar arrives at Juliet's vault to release her, she awakens, realizes that Romeo is dead, and kills herself with his dagger. Rather than be discovered at the scene, the Friar runs away. The next morning, as the play comes to its conclusion, the Friar stands in the churchyard in the presence of the Prince, Montague, and Capulet and repentantly explains all.

> If aught of this
> Miscarried by my fault, let my old life
> Be sacrificed some hour before his time,
> Unto the rigor of severest law.
>
> (V. iii. 266-269)

The last lines of the play belong to the Prince:

> A glooming peace this morning with it brings,
> The sun, for sorrow, will not show his head.
> Go hence to have more talk of these sad things;
> Some shall be pardon'd, and some punished:
> For never was a story of more woe
> Than this of Juliet and her Romeo.
>
> (V. iii. 304-310)

The churchyard is also a garden: a plot of earth designated for burial of the dead. Montague and Capulet agree to have made a "statue in pure gold" (V. iii. 299) of the other's dead child, and to let go of the old enmity that has existed between their families. It would seem that out of the tangled web of deceit the Friar has woven, some good comes, but at what terrible price! In the Friar's soliloquy in the monastery garden he had said, "Virtue itself turn vice, being misapplied, /And vice sometime by action dignified." Those words have proven prophetic of the Friar himself by the end of the play. The Friar's failure to vigilantly garden his own moral life has had tragic implications for the lives of others.

THE GARDEN OF OPHELIA

There are three imaginary gardens in *Hamlet*, if we count as one of them the churchyard burial ground where Hamlet reflects on the skull of Yorick. Another is the orchard in which King Hamlet was sleeping when his brother Claudius murdered him. The orchard itself is not described, but the murder that took place in it is mimed in the dumb show that Hamlet requested the players to perform before Claudius. Another garden, again not described, is the garden from which Ophelia must have gathered the plants that in her state of madness she presents to Laertes, Claudius, and Gertrude.

The plants have symbolic meanings that derive from folk tradition. Two standard works that illumine Shakespeare's uses of the folk symbolism of plants are *Folk Lore of Shakespeare*, by T. F. Thiselton–Dyer (1883), and *The Plant-Lore and Garden-Craft of Shakespeare,* by Henry Nicholson Ellacombe (1884). To Laertes, Ophelia gives rosemary and pansies, associated with remembrance and faithfulness. To Claudius, she gives fennel and columbines. Fennel was a hot herb associated with lust; the columbine, a flower with clustered blossoms, was associated with doves. To Gertrude she gives rue, the "herb of grace" (IV. v. 182), a bitter herb associated with both sorrow and repentance. She gives Gertrude only one daisy, associated with innocence, as though to suggest there is little innocence in Gertrude. When Ophelia gives the rue to Gertrude she saves a sprig for herself. "There's rue for you," she says, "and here's some for me; . . . You may wear your rue with a difference." (IV. v. 181, 183). What is the "difference"? Gertrude should wear her rue in repentance for her adulterous relationship with Claudius, while Ophelia will wear hers in sorrow for the lost attentions of Prince Hamlet and the death of her father Polonius. Mad or deranged she may be, but Ophelia draws on a folk symbolism of plants that is anything except flattering of Claudius and Gertrude.

Did either Claudius or Gertrude catch the meaning of the symbolism? Apparently they did not. There is no hint of resentment in the soulful words Gertrude speaks to Laertes in response to his question about the manner of his sister's death.

> There is a willow grows askaunt the brook,
> That sows his hoary leaves in the glassy stream,
> Therewith fantastic garlands did she make
> Of crow-flowers, nettles, daisies, and long purples
> That liberal shepherds give a grosser name,
> But our cull-cold maids do dead men's fingers call them.
> There on the pendant boughs her crownet weeds
> Clamb'ring to hang, an envious sliver broke,
> When down her weedy trophies and herself
> Fell in weeping brook. Her clothes spread wide,
> And mermaid-like awhile they bore her up,
> Which time she chaunted snatches of old lauds,
> As one incapable of her own distress,
> Or like a creature native and indued
> Unto that element. But long it could not be
> Till that her garments, heavy with their drink
> Pull'd the poor wretch from her melodious lay
> To muddy death.
>
> (IV. vii. 166-183)

The symbolism of plants haunts these lines. The "fantastic garlands" that Ophelia wove are made of "crow-flowers," or buttercups, of "nettles, daisies, and long purples." Reference to these springtime plants provides a symbolic commentary, a kind of obituary, on the brevity, suffering, and innocence of Ophelia's life. Often in Shakespeare we come across sexual imagery. The "long purples" or "dead men's fingers" refer to the dangling tubers of the spring's purple orchid. Shakespeare leaves to the reader's imagination what name shepherds give to the plant. Ophelia's obituary, written in the symbolism of plants, portrays a "cold-cull," or chaste maid, thwarted in her anticipation of married love, absorbed in the witchery of her own singing as she drifts to a watery death.

THE GARDEN OF RICHARD THE SECOND

Richard the Second is one of eight plays that tell of the struggles for the English throne among descendants of Edward the Third. The plays, in the chronological order of the hundred-year history they cover, from the late fourteenth to the late fifteenth centuries, are *Richard the Second; Henry the Fourth, Parts One* and *Two; Henry the Fifth; Henry the Sixth, Parts One, Two,* and *Three; and Richard the Third.*

Richard the Second came to the throne at the age of ten upon the death of his father, Edward the Black Prince, who was the son and heir to the throne of Edward the Third. Until he reached maturity, Richard was a figurehead king. Several councils first directed affairs of government, then a group called the Appellants. Two politically powerful uncles, John of Gaunt and Thomas of Woodstock, had familial oversight of the young Richard. Around age twenty, Richard began to go his own way, surrounding himself with favorites, making political decisions that were not in the best interest of the kingdom. Obsessed with a sense of kingly right, he confiscated properties of nobility, spent lavishly, and imposed burdensome taxes on his people.

Shakespeare derived his information about the life of Richard from several sources, largely from the prose chronicles of Edward Hall and Raphael Holinshed, but he manipulated the information for dramatic purposes. For instance, Richard first married Anne of Bohemia. Both were age fifteen. She died of plague in 1394. In 1396, when Richard was age twenty-nine, he parlayed a peace with France by marrying Isabella, the seven-year-old daughter of the French King. In the play, Richard's mature queen, his second spouse, is a dramatic invention. Shakespeare selectively and imaginatively drew on those features of Richard's life that would make good box office. He picked up on Richard's life when Richard was at the peak of his power, and dramatized the trajectory of events that led to Richard's downfall. The play is not history, but for many of the people in Shakespeare's audience it was the only history of Richard's life and reign they would have known.

There is an imaginary garden in the play in which the Queen and her two attendants eavesdrop on two gardeners who are discussing Richard's misrule of his kingdom. Richard has exiled his cousin, Bullingbrook, son of John of Gaunt, whom Richard has perceived as a threat to his crown. While Richard is away from England on an ego-driven venture to whip Irish Lords into political submission, Bullingbrook has returned from exile in France, drawn together an army, and has Richard and his military allies on the verge of defeat. While the gardeners converse, the first gardener says to the second,

Go bind up young dangling apricocks,
Which like unruly children make their sire
Stoop with oppression of their prodigal weight;

Give some supportance to the bending twigs.
Go thou, and like an executioner
Cut off the heads of [too] fast growing sprays,
That look too lofty in our commonwealth;
All must be even in our government.
You thus employed, I will go root away
The noisome weeds which without profit suck
The soil's fertility from wholesome flowers.

(III. iv. 29-39)

The second gardener replies:

Why should we in the compass of a pale
Keep law and form and due proportion,
Showing as in a model our firm estate,
When our sea-walled garden, the whole land,
Is full of weeds, her fairest flowers chok'd up,
Her fruit-trees all unprun'd, her hedges ruin'd,
Her knots disordered, and her wholesome herbs
Swarming with caterpillars?

(III. iv. 40-47)

The first gardener says:

Hold thy peace.
He that hath suffered this disordered spring
Hath now himself met with the fall of leaf.
The weeds which his broad-spreading leaves did shelter
That seem'd in eating him to hold him up,
Are pluck'd up root and all by Bullingbrook . . . .

(III. iv. 48-52)

O, what pity is it
That he had not so trimm'd and dress'd his land
As we this garden! [We] at time of year
Do wound the bark, the skin of our fruit-trees,
Lest being over-proud in sap and blood,
With too much riches it confound itself;
Had he done so to great and growing men,
They might have liv'd to bear and he to taste
Their fruits of duty. Superfluous branches
We lop away, that bearing boughs may live;
Had he done so himself had borne the crown,
Which waste of idle hours hath quite thrown down.

(III. iv. 55-66)

The second gardener asks:

What, think you the King shall be deposed?

(III. iv. 67)

The first gardener answers:

Depress'd he is already, and depos'd
'Tis doubt he will be.

(III. iv. 68-69)

Shocked at what she overhears, the Queen steps out from her hiding place among the shadow of trees and rebukes the first gardener in biblical imagery.

Thou old Adam's likeness, set to dress this garden,
How dares thy harsh rude tongue sound this unpleasing news?

What Eve, what serpent, hath suggested thee
To make a second fall of cursed man?
Why dost thou say King Richard is depos'd?
Dar'st thou, thou little better thing than earth,
Divine his downfall?

(III. iv. 77-79)

Shakespeare's imaginary garden in *Richard the Second* is a transplanting of the biblical Garden of Eden onto the "sea-walled" garden of Richard's kingdom. Shakespeare locates the model for Richard's rule in the biblical Adam. Like Adam, Richard failed to keep the garden kingdom it was his to keep.

The play appeared in 1597 in the politically uncertain climate of Elizabeth's declining years. She objected to the play for the reason that it dealt with the dethronement of a monarch. She complained to a visitor at her court, "I am Richard II. Know ye not that?"[2] Who knows if Shakespeare had any intent of drawing a comparison between Elizabeth and Richard. The play reaches beyond the specifics of history to say something that is timeless and applicable to persons in all walks of life: keep the garden that your station in life requires you to keep.

THE GARDEN OF LORENZO AND JESSICA

We live in a vastly different culture from Shakespeare's, but for all the industrial, material, and technological advantages we pay a price. We have spent years in the glare of electric lights by night, but are far less familiar with the lights of the heavens than Shakespeare or the lowliest peasants of the fields would have been. So what have we lost? The ability to discern the coming and the passing of the seasons by the stars is of no particular consequence in our culture. We have calendars, watches, and cell phones that inform us of time. But the culture we have constructed cuts us off from a former sense of the spinning heavens, of the universe as a slow wheel of time. If we lose that sense of the universe, and the wonder it evoked, we have lost connection with a spiritual universe to which people of Shakespeare's culture would have thought human existence to be related. Were they right that human existence is related to a spiritual universe? Are we right to neglect that possibility?

An imaginary garden in Shakespeare that points symbolically to the realm of spirit is near the conclusion of *The Merchant of Venice*. The two lovers, Lorenzo and Jessica, are sitting under the night sky. She has abandoned the household of her overbearing father to elope with Lorenzo and to face an uncertain future as a Jew united with a Christian. Jessica remarks on the music that musicians are playing in the background. It strangely troubles her. Lorenzo explains that the effect the music is having on her is a sign of music's miraculous power. He elaborates in the following words:

> The reason is, your spirits are attentive;
> For do but note a wild and wanton herd
> Or race of youthful and unhandled colts,
> Fetching mad bounds, bellowing and neighing loud,
> Which is the hot condition of their blood,
> If they but hear perchance a trumpet sound,
> Or any air of music touch their ears,
> You shall perceive them make a mutual stand,
> Their savage eyes turn'd to a modest gaze,
> By the sweet power of music; therefore the poet
> Did feign that Orpheus drew trees, stones, and floods;
> Since nought so stockish, hard, and full of rage,
> But music for the time doth change his nature.

The man that hath no music in himself,
Nor is not moved with concord of sweet sounds,
Is fit for treasons, stratagems, and spoils;
The motions of his spirit are dull as night,
And his affections dark as [Erebus]:
Let no such man be trusted. Mark the music.

(V. i. 70-88)

What is this music? It is the natural music of the spheres. Lorenzo's words recall the Pythagorean notion that the physical planets give off musical sounds as they turn about the earth. Lorenzo suggests that the goal of human life is to realize within oneself this celestial harmony. Within us is a spirit that when finely tuned to the music of the spheres finds itself in harmony with the Governing Spirit of the universe.

So far as I can tell there is nothing superfluous in Shakespeare's writing. His imaginary gardens confront readers with profusions of natural imagery. Readers might gloss over this imagery as being merely "flowery" writing, or they might consider its philosophical suggestiveness. I have suggested that the imagery associated with Friar Lawrence is moral; the imagery associated with Ophelia is both erotic and funereal; the imagery associated with Richard is political; and the imagery associated with Lorenzo and Jessica is metaphysical.

Leo Tolstoy in a famous essay claimed that Shakespeare's literary reputation was overrated. He might have entertained, but he did not offer "the teaching of life."[3] Does Shakespeare offer the teaching of life? When I sit in my garden on a summer's evening, I recall the words of Lorenzo to Jessica. My ear is not keen enough to hear the music of the spheres, but I do not doubt the possibility that it exists. In fact, I imagine I hear it imitated in the vibrant sounds emitted by the hosts of creatures that occupy the garden with me. When I think how I "rule" in my relations with others, I recall the misrule of Richard. When I think how emotionally traumatic love can be, I recall the madness of Ophelia and the pathos of her death. And when I think of the noxious weeds in my own moral garden, I think of the truancy of Friar Lawrence. Imaginary gardens are spaces in Shakespeare's plays that invite us to enter as attentive participants, and to reflect on the garden conditions of our own lives.

NOTES

1. Quotations from Shakespeare are from *The Riverside Shakespeare*, ed. G. Blakemore Evans (Boston: Houghton Mifflin Company, 1974).

2. Michael Wood, *In Search of Shakespeare* (London: BBC Books, 2005), 257.

3. Leo Tolstoy, *Tolstoy on Shakespeare: A Critical Essay on Shakespeare*, trans. V. Tchertkoff and I. F. M. Gloucester (United Kingdom: Dodo Press, n.d.), 62.

9

R. S. Thomas: Poet of the Creation

We know that the world is, in effect, a text, and that it speaks to us, humbly and joyfully, of its own emptiness, but also of the presence of someone else, namely its Creator.

—Paul Claudel, *Positions et Propositions*

R ONALD STUART THOMAS was born in Cardiff, Wales in 1913 (died 2000), educated in classics at University College, Bangor, and in theology at St. Michael's College, Llandâf. After taking orders, he served the Anglican Church in Wales for over forty years. In retirement, looking back over his clerical career, Thomas said, "As long as I was a priest of the Church, I felt an obligation to try to present the Bible message in a more or less orthodox way. I never felt that I was employed by the Church to preach my own . . . questionings."[1] It was Thomas's portion in life to be a Christian clergyman at a time in the history of Western culture when previously accepted authority of the church has dwindled. In his work we find indifferent parishioners, half-empty churches, and despairing clergymen. Thomas may not have expressed his "questionings" in his sermons, but he did express them in his highly autobiographical poetry and prose.

In 1936, fresh from theological studies, newly ordained, and unmarried, Thomas accepted his first post as curate of Chirk, a mining village on the Welsh-English border. In Chirk he met Mildred Eldridge ("Elsie"), a painter, whom he married in 1940. That year, Thomas became curate of a parish in Hanmer. He did not have much choice about his place of work as a curate, but as a prospective rector he chose his first parish at Manafon, which he served from 1942 to 1954. After Manafon, he served a parish at Eglwysfach until 1967; and after Eglwysfach a parish at Aberdaron until his retirement in 1978. Thomas published fifteen books of poetry while serving these three parishes. These and the books of poetry he wrote after his retirement are conveniently collected in two paperback volumes.[2]

AT MANAFON

At Manafon, Thomas published the poems in *The Stones in the Field* (1946), *An Acre of Land* (1952), *The Minister* (1953), and many of the later poems in the collection, *Song at the Year's Turning* (1955). He said that when he went to Manafon he "was brought up hard against this community and . . . really began to learn what . . . rural human nature was like." "And I must say," he continues, "that I found nothing I'd been told in theological college was of any help at all in these circumstances."[3]

In one of the longest poems he wrote, Thomas assumes the persona of a nonconformist clergyman who comes up hard against a rural community. Broadcast on the Welsh Regional Programme of the BBC in 1952, *The Minister* is a verse drama with four characters: the narrator, Davies, the Minister, and Buddug. The first six lines describe the setting of the poem, where the narrator says:

> In the hill country at the moor's edge
> There is a chapel, religion's outpost
> In the untamed land west of the valleys,
> The marginal land where flesh meets spirit
> Only on Sundays and the days between
> Are mortgaged to the grasping soil
>
> ("The Minister," *CP*, 42)

The young clergyman who comes to serve the chapel, Elias Morgan, B. A., learns early that the people have not hired him to preach Christian love. Words about love

>   are blown
> To pieces by the unchristened wind
> In the chapel rafters. . . .
>
> ("The Minister," *CP* 42)

The people of the chapel choose their pastors, as they choose their horses, by their capacity for hard work. That work is hard in ways Morgan could not have imagined. He offers a Bible class but no one comes except Mali, who is "not right in the head" and has a "passion" for him (*CP*, 49). Job Davies, chief elder of the chapel and the wealthiest man in the community, flirts during the service with the simple maid, Buddug, who imagines Davies will leave his old wife to marry her. When Morgan admonishes Davies about this flirtation, Davies tells him to keep his nose

> In the Black Book, so it won't be tempted
> To go sniffing where it's not wanted
> And leave us farmers to look to our own
> Business.
>
> ("The Minister," *CP*, 51)

By the end of the poem, disillusionment has replaced Morgan's earlier enthusiasm for serving the people of the parish. His mind

> Fester[s] with brooding on the sly
> Infirmities of the hill people.
>
> ("The Minister," CP, 54)

A fundamental problem Thomas wrestled with at Manafon was how to overcome a complicated system of spiritual and cultural barriers that stood between him and his rural parishioners. Speaking of these parishioners, he writes:

> They were hard-working and narrow, with the crude wisdom of workers on the land. Theirs was mixed farming, so they had little time for cultural pursuits. . . . Any of my enthusiastic expressions about the beauty of the surrounding country were met with faint smiles, half-amused, half-cynical. Yet they loved the land in their own way, and were prepared to talk about it for hours, when I visited them of an evening. One of the subjects to avoid was

religion, [though] they liked to entertain the Rector and his wife to supper."[4]

One afternoon, while returning home from a pastoral visit to a hill-top farm, Thomas saw the farmer's brother working in a beet field. From that visit he found inspiration to write the first of eighteen poems spread over several books about Iago Prytherch, Thomas's "symbol of the hill farmer."[5]

Prytherch is

> Just an ordinary man of the bald Welsh hills,
> Who pens a few sheep in a gap of cloud.
> Docking mangels, chipping the green skin
> From the yellow bones with a half-witted grin
> Of satisfaction.

Thomas observes that "There is something frightening in the vacancy of [Prytherch's] mind." "This is your prototype," he declares,

> who, season by season
> Against siege of rain and the wind's attrition,
> Preserves his stock, an impregnable fortress
> Not to be stormed even in death's confusion.
> ("A Peasant," *The Stones of the Field*, *CP*, 4)

Thomas rails at people like Prytherch:

> Men of the hills, wantoners, men of Wales,
> With your sheep and your pigs and your ponies, your sweaty females,
> How I have hated you for your irreverence, your scorn even

Of the refinements of art and the mysteries of the Church.
("A Priest to His People, *The Stones of the Field, CP,* 13)

In spite of his railing, he wonders if the mysteries of the church he offers to these people can compete with an instinctive, natural religion they already have. He asks of himself,

Is there anything to show that your essential need
Is less than his who has the world for church.
And stands bare-headed in the woods' wide porch
Morning and evening to hear God's choir
Scatter their praises?
"Affinity, *The Stones of the Field,*" *CP,* 8.)

During his Manfon years, Thomas questioned not just the effectiveness of his ministry in relation to the people he served, but even its relevance.

AT EGLWYSFACH

When Thomas moved from Manafon to Eglwysfach in 1954, he exchanged a parish in east Wales for one on the Irish Sea in the west. To his thirteen years at Eglwysfach belong four books of poetry: *Poetry for Supper* (1958), *Tares* (1961), *The Bread of Truth* (1963), and *Pietà.* (1966).

Eglwysfach was a rural village well into Welsh speaking Wales. A devoted nationalist, Thomas had laboriously learned Welsh to be able to communicate in that tongue. But because of its proximity to the cultural center of Aberystwyth—with its University College and the National Library of Wales—Eglwysfach was attractive to English speaking retirees of little or no Welsh ancestry who made up the stronger part of Thomas's congregation.[6] He was frustrated at having to conduct services mostly in English. And there were obviously

other frustrations. We hear him complain that he is among that anti-
quated group of

> Venerable men, their black cloth
> A little dusty, a little green
> With holy mildew.
>> ("The Country Clergy," *Poetry for Supper, CP, 82*)

The routine of parish affairs prompts him to think back to

> an earlier self, to summon
> To the mind's hearth, as I would now,
> You, Prytherch, there to renew
> The lost poetry of our talk
> Over embers of that world
> We built together: not built either,
> But found lingering on the farm
> As sun lingers about the corn
> That in the stackyard makes its own light.
>> ("Temptation of a Poet," *Poetry for Supper, CP,* 73.)

He cannot think of Prytherch without questioning his own way of
life, and feeling repentant that he ever judged Prytherch's.

> Prytherch, man, can you forgive
> From your stone altar on which the light's
> Bread is broken at dusk and dawn
> One who strafed you with thin scorn
> From the cheap gallery of his mind?
>> ("Absolution," *Poetry for Supper, CP, 92*)

Thomas underwent a period of personal theological questioning in his years at Eglwysfach. He wrote poems about nature, individual persons, rural life, and Welsh nationalism, but especially noteworthy for their theological questioning are the poems "Amen," "Service," "In Church," and "The Belfry." In "The Belfry," he writes:

> I have seen it standing up grey,
> Gaunt, as though no sunlight
> Could ever thaw out the music
> Of its great bell: terrible
> In its own way, for religion
> Is like that. There are times
> When a black frost is upon
> One's whole being, and the heart
> In its bone belfry hangs and is dumb.
>
> ("The Belfry," *Pietà*, *CP*, 168)

The Welsh philosopher D. Z. Phillips speaks of Thomas as a modern poet of the *deus absconditus*, the God who hides himself.[7] During the Eglwysfach years, Thomas came to terms with the idea of waiting on a God who is remote and mute. There is no better commentator on this idea of waiting than Thomas himself. "God, reality, whatever it is," he said, "is not going to be forced, it's not going to be put to question, it works in its own time. . . . And out of this . . . comes the feeling that perhaps this is all one is required to do. It's the Milton idea, isn't it, they also serve who only stand and wait."[8]

If in his sermons Thomas hinted at the idea of waiting on God, he must have caused raised eyebrows among his parishioners. After all, if the pastor is not on immediate terms with the Lord, then who is? In "The Mill," the speaker is a clergyman who is attending a dying parishioner:

I called of an evening,
Watched how the lamp
Explored the contours
Of his face's map.
On the wall his shadow
Grew stern as he talked
Of the old exploits
With plough, and scythe.
I read him the psalms,
Said prayers and was still.

. . . .

Nine years in that bed
From season to season
The great frame rotted,
While the past's slow stream,
Flowing through his head,
Kept the rusty mill
Of the mind turning—
It was I it ground.

("The Mill," The Bread of Truth, CP, 144-45)

A striking feature of these lines is the clergyman's stillness, or stoical acceptance, of the brute finality of death. Rarely in his poetry does Thomas proclaim the good news of Easter. What are we to make of a poem like "The Mill," however, in which he intimates there is no good news to proclaim?

AT ABERDARON

In 1967, with the move from Eglwysfach to a parish at Aberdaron, Thomas found a community that was to his liking. Aberdaron was a small fishing village on the end of the peninsula of Llŷn, inhabited by farmers, fishermen, and sailors. Three miles out to sea was the island of Bardsey, noted for its ornithological observatory, where Thomas could indulge his passion for bird watching. And since Welsh was the first language of many of the inhabitants of the village, Thomas was free to communicate in that language.[9]

During his twelve years at Aberdaron, Thomas published seven books of poetry: *Not That He Brought Flowers* (1968), *Young and Old* (1972), *H'm* (1972), *What is a Welshman?* (1974), *Laboratories of the Spirit* (1975), *The Way of It* (1977), and *Frequencies* (1978). Prytherch no longer frequents these poems, yet there is reminiscence of a primal relationship with the world of nature that Thomas associated with Prytherch.

In the following lines, Thomas imagines himself a second Adam who looks upon the world of nature for the first time.

God looked at space and I appeared,
Rubbing my eyes at what I saw.
. . . .
    As though born again
I stepped out into the cool dew. . .
. . . .
Astonished at the mingled chorus
Of weeds and flowers. In the brown bark
Of the Trees I saw the many faces
Of life, forms hungry for birth,
Mouthing at me. I held my way
To the light, inspecting my shadow
Boldly; and in the late morning
You, rising towards me out of the depths
Of myself. I took your hand

Remembering you, and together,
Confederates of the natural day,
We went forth to meet the Machine.

("Once," *H'M, CP, 208*)

The "Machine" is Thomas's customary metaphor for the science and technology he saw as destructive of traditional patterns of life. But who is the "You" of the poem? It could be a reference to Eve; it could be a familiar way of addressing God; or it could be, as I suggest it is, a reference to a former self that rises to the surface of Thomas's consciousness as he recalls past experiences he has had in relation to the world of nature.

One of those past experiences he records in the essay "Two Chapels," published in 1948. He tells of venturing into the countryside alone to visit two ancient chapels. At one of these chapels, finding the door locked, he stretched out on the grass and let his mind wander:

As with St. John the Divine on the island of Patmos I was "in the Spirit" and I had a vision, in which I could comprehend the breadth and length and depth and height of the mystery of the creation. But I won't try to put the experience into words. It would be impossible. I will simply say that I realized there was really no such thing as time, no beginning and no end but that everything is a fountain welling up endlessly from immortal God. There was certainly something in the place that gave me this feeling. The chapel stood in the fields, amidst the waving grass, its roof covered with a layer of yellow lichen. There were tall nettles growing around and at its side there swayed a big old tree like someone leaning forward to listen to the sermon. It was therefore easy to believe that I was living centuries ago. It might have been the first day of Creation and myself one of the first men. Might have been? No it *was* the first day. The world was recreated before my eyes. The dew of its creation was on everything, and I fell to my knees and praised God—a young man worshipping a young God, for surely that is what our God is.[10]

With his retirement in 1978, Thomas was glad to be free of customary ministerial duties. He and his wife Elsie retreated to an ancient stone cottage in Sarn on the far southwest coast of Wales. Of that locale, he says,

> Here I can watch the night sky,
> listen to how one grass blade
> grates on another as member
> of a disdained orchestra.
> . . . .
> No longer guilty of wasting
> my time, I take my place
> by a lily-flower, believing
> with Blake that when God comes
>
> he comes sometimes by way
> of the nostril.
>
> ("Retired," *Mass for Hard Times, CLP,* 147)

The speaker of these lines seems hardly the same one who spoke dispiritedly of waiting on God. In his "Autobiographical Essay," published in his retirement, Thomas speaks of how he has come to understand the calling of his life and work.

It would seem that the deity has chosen to mediate himself to me via the world, or even the universe, of nature. I realize . . . because I have chosen the love of created things, I may not have reached the highest state possible to a human here on earth, but must be content with the fact that that is the sort of poet I am.[11]

Among created things that Thomas loved were the non-human creatures that fill the earth. He loved looking at them, studying them, marveling at the individuality of their being. In "Bestiary," he observes that "the Owl has a clock's face"; the whiskers of mice "are finer than the strings of a violin"; the mosquito is a miniature "crane"; the snake has "doll's eyes": the goat has "A glass eye"; the tiger at the zoo has a "concertina face"; the bear is "cuddly" but also fierce; and the lizard is a "trigger cocked on the sunned stone in readiness to go off." (*CLP*, 272-75).

Most of all, Thomas loved birds. In his autobiography *No-One*, he draws a correspondence between bird watching and prayer. Writing in the third person, he says:

Spending an hour or two looking over the sea hoping to see a migratory bird, he came to see the similarity between this and praying. He had to wait patiently for a long time for fear of losing the rare bird, because he did not now when it would come by. It is exactly the same with the relationship between man and God that is known as prayer. Great patience is called for, because no one knows when God will choose to reveal Himself.[12]

Despite his questionings about the *deus absconditis*—the God who hides himself—the authority of the church in modern western culture, and his personal role as a minister within the church, Thomas speaks from within the biblical tradition that nourished him. He lifts up a basic question that is at the heart of that tradition: where and how is God known? There were no synagogues prior to Abraham, nor were there churches prior to Christ. Does the creation reveal knowledge of God?

Thomas over the course of his career as a clergyman and poet reached a theological conclusion that is aptly expressed by the theologian John Baillie: "The knowledge of God which we have on earth is of a kind that we cannot conceive to exist apart from some knowledge of things."[13] God and the creation are not identical, but earthly things are luminous of their Creator. Thomas's poetic work proclaims, with the Psalmist, "The heavens declare the glory of God; and the firmament sheweth his handywork."[14]

Notes

1. R. S. Thomas, "R. S. Thomas: Autobiographical Essay," *Miraculous Simplicity*, ed. William V. Davis (Fayetteville: The University of Arkansas Press, 1993), 17.

2. *R. S. Thomas: Collected Poems 1945-1990* (London: Phoenix Orion House, 1993); and *R. S. Thomas: Collected Later Poems: 1988-2000* (Northumberland: Bloodaxe Books Ltd., 2013). These are the volumes I use in discussing Thomas' poetry. I designate where the poems appear in these two collections by titles of the books in which the poems originally appeared, and, by page numbers where quotations from the poems appear in the two collections, noted as *CP*, for *Collected Poems*, and *CLP* for *Collected Later Poems*.

3. "R. S. Thomas: Priest and Poet," transcript of John Ormand's film for BBC television, broadcast 2 April 1972. *Poetry Wales* (Spring 1972), 49.

4. Thomas, "Autobiographical Essay," *Miraculous Simplicity*, 10.

5. Thomas, "Autobiographical Essay," *Miraculous Simplicity*, 9-10.

6. Thomas, "Autobiographical Essay," *Miraculous Simplicity*, 13.

7. D. Z. Phillips, *R. S. Thomas: Poet of the Hidden God* (London: The Macmillan Press Ltd., 1986).

8. Transcript, "R. S. Thomas: Priest and Poet," 51.

9. Thomas, "Autobiographical Essay," *Miraculous Simplicity*, 16.

10. *R. S. Thomas,* "Two Chapels," *Selected Prose*, ed. Sandra Anstey (Bridgend: Poetry of Wales Press, 1986), 44.

11. Thomas, "Autobiographical Essay," *Miraculous Simplicity*, 19.

12. R. S. Thomas, *No-One, R. S. Thomas Autobiographies*, trans. from the Welsh, with an introduction and notes, by Jason Walford Davies (London: J. M. Dent, 1997), 100.

13. Donald Baillie, *Our Knowledge of God* (New York: Charles Scribner's Sons, 1959), 179.

14. Ps. 19: 1.

10

ANN LEE, FREDERICK WILLIAM EVANS, AND THE SHAKER VISION OF HEAVEN ON EARTH

Ah, but man's reach should exceed his grasp, Or what's a heaven for?

—ROBERT BROWNING, "ANDREA DEL SARTO"

I N 1774, A party of eight people from England came to America who were seeking relief from religious persecution. These eight were the forerunners of the Shaker religion. As an organized religious movement, Shakerism, formally called the United Society of Believers in Christ's Second Appearing, is now greatly diminished from what it once was. At the height of its development in the mid-nineteenth century, Shakerism had about 6000 resident members in eighteen communitarian settlements that stretched from southern Kentucky to Maine. At the end of the twentieth century, the few remaining resident Shakers lived in two settlements: one at Sabbathday Lake in Maine, the other at Canterbury in New Hampshire. In the twenty–first century, Sabbathday Lake is the last of the Shaker settlements where a form of Shakerism is practiced.

In the early years of their existence, the outer world ridiculed and persecuted the Shakers for such features of their religion as millenarianism, communism, pacifism, celibacy, and charismatic worship. In later years, the outer world's attitude gradually shifted to one of appreciation, especially of the perfectionist qualities of Shaker craftsmanship. The Trappist monk Thomas Merton famously said, "The peculiar grace of a Shaker chair is due to the fact that it was made by someone capable of believing that an angel might come and sit on it."[1] A Shaker woman's oblique rejoinder to Merton's remark was that she did not "want to be remembered as a piece of furniture."[2] Behind the chair, as behind the Shaker way of life generally, was a religion dedicated to building a heaven on earth.

The founding matriarch of the Shakers, Mother Ann Lee, could neither read nor write. She had a powerful gift of expression, however, that enabled her to present a practical vision of what was wrong with human society as well as a vision of a better world to live in. Immediately after her death in 1784, Ann Lee's followers, Joseph Meacham and Lucy Wright, took up her work and established Shaker beliefs and practices in the gathered communities. Within these communities over succeeding generations, a host of writers of varying levels of education and literary skill drew out the implications of Ann Lee's vision in treatises, journals, diaries, letters, poetry, and pamphlets. Shaker writings convey a dissident form of Protestantism that repudiated the possibility of any creed or confession as a test of faith, and excluded the Scriptures as a fixed form of revelation. Because statements of what the Shakers believed varied over time, "no one individual or text can be proposed as the authentic Shaker statement."[3] No individual among Shaker writers was a brighter intellect or possessed a surer literary skill than Frederick William Evans. His *Autobiography of a Shaker* affords access to what the Shakers believed from the standpoint of a venerated Elder who near the end of the nineteenth century looked back over the course of Shaker history.

Evans, born in Leominster, England in 1808, immigrated at twelve years old to America with his father and brother. In America, he took an interest in books and learning and immersed himself in the socialistic theories of Robert Owen and Charles Fourier. Along with his brother, George, he worked to publish *The Workingman's Advocate, The Daily Sentinel,* and *Young America.* At the masthead of *Young America* the two brothers printed the twelve planks of their platform: The right of man to the soil; Down with monopolies, especially the United States Bank; Freedom of the public lands; Homesteads made inalienable; Abolition of all laws for the collection of debts; A general bankrupt law; A lien of the laborer upon his own work for his wages; Abolition of imprisonment for debt; Equal rights of women with men in all respects; Abolition of chattel slavery and wage slavery; Land limitation to 160 acres [per lifetime of the individual]; and Mails to run on the Sabbath.[4]

In 1828, Evans set out in search of an established community where he could put into practice his socialistic convictions. That search led him in 1830 to the Shaker community at New Lebanon, New York. At the time of this visit Evans was a materialist and professed atheist; but the candor, openness, and contentment of the Shakers inclined him toward belief in the existence of a spiritual sphere. The final evidence for this spiritual sphere came to Evans through a personal experience. He describes in his *Autobiography of a Shaker* an encounter with "angels" who appeared to him at New Lebanon as he reclined on his bed. They showed me, he says, "the facts of the existence of a spiritual world, of the immortality of the human soul, and of the possibility and reality of intercommunication between souls in and spirits out of the mortal body."[5] Evans concluded, "that there really was a God,"[6] and that revelation, or communication, existed between God and humans as much in the present time as in biblical times.

Over the remainder of his life of eighty-five years, Evans (died 1893), through his public lectures and published writings, became the chief spokesman for Shakerism to the outer world. He was an exponent of women's rights; a vegetarian who moralized on the health hazards of meat, tobacco, and alcohol; an advocate—on Malthusian grounds—of celibacy as a way to control population growth; and an abolitionist. In an interview with Lincoln, he argued the principle of non-resistance and persuaded the President to exempt Shaker men from the Civil War draft. He also carried on private correspondence with international figures such as Henry George and Leo Tolstoy. Indeed, in a response to one of Evans's letters, the Russian novelist turned-social-reformer indicated that he had read and derived "spiritual nourishment"[7] from the writings of Evans and other Shaker authors. Evans's *Autobiography* contains the essence of his writing. In November of 1868, he was a delegate to a Shaker missionary convention in Boston. As an offshoot of this convention, a friend, J. T. Fields, asked him to write "'an autobiographical account of [his] experience as a seeker after truth.'"[8] The *Autobiography* first appeared in two parts in the 1869 April and May issues of the *Atlantic Monthly*. Later the same year, he reissued the text in book form; and again in book form in 1888. The enlarged 1888 edition—which Porcupine Press reprinted in 1972—included writings of fellow Shakers along with generous extracts from Evans' previously published writings.

Evans suggests in the Preface that he is writing the *Autobiography* to defend Shakerism against those who think it is "the extreme of ignorance and fanaticism . . , [a religion] entirely outside the pale of philosophical and logical investigation"[9] This suggestion is misleading, however, because he is hardly offering a systematic defense of Shakerism. He is offering, instead, a testimony to the progress of his own spiritual life within Shakerism, the purpose of which is to incline others to follow in his footsteps and to become Shakers. Quoting himself from a previous conversational context, he declares, "If I can reach such a baptism [of faith], no other human being need doubt the possibility of a like attainment"[10] After the first thirty-four pages of his 271 page book, Evans ceases to focus on the details of his own life to focus instead on what he offers as the core of the Shaker religion: its "Plan of Salvation."[11]

He begins his description of the Shaker Plan of Salvation with an idealizing portrait of Ann Lee. She was born in 1736 in Manchester, England, one of eight children of a poor blacksmith and a pious mother. "She was not like other children," Evans insists, "addicted to play, but was serious and thoughtful. She was early the subject of religious impressions, and was often favoured with heavenly visions."[12]

But she *was* like other children of her social class in the sense that economic circumstances forced her to go to work instead of going to school: first in a cotton factory, then a hatter's shop, and finally in the kitchen of an infirmary.

As she grew older, Ann Lee had a deepening sense of the depravity of human nature and especially of the depravity of the human sexual act. Despite her pleadings with her parents, they forced her into marriage with a blacksmith, Abraham Stanley, by whom she had four children. Ann Lee construed the early deaths of these children as punishment for her sexual experience. Her "excessive tribulation of soul," Evans reports, caused her to spend "whole nights in labouring and crying to God to open some way of salvation."[13]

In 1758, Ann Lee joined a group of former Quakers that had been influenced by Camisards, French Protestants who claimed to have prophetic visions. Gradually she became the leader of this group and persuaded them to accept celibacy as a sign of following Christ. People of Manchester, England were hostile toward the strange methods of worship—dancing and shaking—and the zealous evangelizing of the people with whom Ann Lee was associated. What right had a woman to preach against the biblical command to multiply and replenish the earth? In 1770, in conjunction with an extended period of imprisonment in Manchester for disturbing the peace, Ann Lee "saw Jesus Christ in open vision, who revealed to her the most astonishing views and divine manifestations of truth." From that time forward, Evans says, "she was received by the people as a mother in spiritual things, and was thenceforth by them called Mother Ann."[14]

In a lengthy interpretation of the Book of Revelation, Evans maintains that Ann Lee is key to unlocking the book's symbolism. When Revelation speaks of the Son of Man, Evans insists, it is not referring exclusively to Jesus. In the things of nature is a manifestation of two great fundamental principles, male and female. Since God is the cause of all things, it reasonably follows that God must be male and female. The Eastern world has stressed the male side of divinity in such figures as Zoroaster of Persia, Confucius of China, Brahman of India, and Jesus of Judea. The Western world, on the other hand, is now beginning, within the Shaker religion, to stress the female side of divinity in the figure of Ann Lee. She is the "Daughter of Man"[15] who has "gathered around her a 'cloud of witnesses,' clothed in white raiment--righteousness--and now sits upon it as her throne of glory."[16]

According to the Shaker Plan of Salvation, as Evans renders it, Mother Ann is "Ann Christ,"[17] the female complement to Jesus Christ. She is a person in a special manner possessed of the Divine Spirit and adopted by God as his daughter. Mother Ann represents the second appearance prophesied in the Book of Revelation, the second manifestation of the Spirit of God in human history, just as Jesus Christ represents the first manifestation. With Mother Ann, Revelation's prophecy of the millennium has begun. By virtue of her adoption by God, Mother Ann reveals by example of her life and teachings the possibility of attaining a life of purity and contentment, a life of heaven on earth, preparatory of Revelation's assurance of life in the heavenly city of the New Jerusalem.

At the time Evans wrote his *Autobiography*, Shakerism as a practiced religion had passed its peak. After the Civil War the membership fell off so dramatically that by the mid-1870s the United Society had resorted to advertising for new members. In 1874, the Shaker community where Evans lived placed the following advertisement in several New York newspapers:

Men, women, and children can find a comfortable home for life, where want never comes, with the Shakers, by embracing

the true faith and living pure lives. Particulars can be learned
by writing to the Shakers, Mount Lebanon, New York.[18]

Evans undertook two unproductive trips to England to recruit new
members to Shakerism, the first in 1871, the second in 1887. His
proselytizing activities, both through his travels and writings, were
among the last great efforts of the Shakers to attract the world to the
religion of Mother Ann.

I sift from the writing of the scholar of Shakerism Edward
Andrews[19] three main factors that led to the decline of the Shakers.
One was their practice of celibacy. They adopted orphans and
opened their doors to converts and strangers, but they bore no children to carry the religion forward. A second factor was economics. The Shakers drew converts from economically stressed families
and individuals who were seeking "a comfortable home for life" (see
the quoted advertisement above). Following the Civil War, with the
opening of the West, and the expansion of the Industrial Revolution,
persons who might otherwise have taken up the Shaker religion and
communal life looked independently to economic opportunities in
the national economy at large. A third factor that led to the decline
of the Shakers was the passing of old believers and founders who
knew Ann Lee and kept her memory and teachings alive. With their
passing, the original inspiration of the religion waned. Conversions
continued, but fewer and fewer were able to share the enthusiasm or
were willing to subject themselves to the discipline that the Shaker
religion required of its followers.

Evans' *Autobiography* is a curious mixture of autobiography, biography, and theology. Autobiographically, he speaks about himself;
biographically, he speaks about Ann Lee; theologically, he speaks
about Mother Ann. To most people now, I imagine, the theological
dimension of Evans' work defies credibility. In light of the global

human atrocities and environmental devastations of the twentieth and twenty-first centuries, it appears impossible that Ann Lee as Mother Ann represented the beginning of the biblical millennium. But the Ann Lee of the biographical dimension of Evans' *Autobiography* bears consideration as a charismatic woman of history whose teachings have relevance for our time.

The *Precepts of Mother Ann Lee* is a book of testimonies by witnesses who knew Ann Lee in the flesh and preserved her spoken teachings. Nowhere is recorded in the *Precepts* that she personally claimed the status of divinity that Evans a hundred years after her death claimed for her. She did claim a personal, ecstatic intimacy with divinity, as when she said, "I have been with God and Christ, and I saw the holy angels and heard them sing; and they sang *'Glory to God and the Lamb.'"*[20] Her fundamental teachings, as recorded in the *Precepts,* are those of a woman who bore the wisdom of Gospel teachings in her heart, and impressed them on her followers in her own idiom. I quote from her teachings by page numbers as they appear in the *Precepts*:

—"Put your hands to work and your hearts to God." (208)
—"You ought to be industrious and prudent, and not live a sumptuous and gluttonous life; but labor for a meek and quiet spirit." (209)
—"You must be faithful with your hands, that you may have something to give to the poor; and walk ye uprightly like men of God." (211-12)
—"You ought to love one another, and never have one hard feeling toward each other, but live together every day as though it was the last day you had to live in this world." (215)
—"You are heating yourselves by the fire, while others are shivering in the cold. This is not right." (225)

—"It is a sin to waste soap, or any thing else that God has given you." (226)

—"Do all your work as though you had a thousand years to live, and as you would if you knew you must die to-morrow." (243)

—"You must be kind to strangers." (243)

—"You must not be so down in your feelings, you must walk sharp; and if you think you do as well as your can, you must take faith, and labor to do better; this is the way for you to gain strength." (247)

—"If you labor for [the gift of vision], you shall have it." (248)

These teachings of Ann Lee, as did the teachings of Jesus of the Gospels, encourage in affairs of living the practices of industry, prudence, thrift, humility, charity, neighborliness, forgiveness, vigilance, and optimism, all in the interest of creating a better world to live in, even a heaven on earth.

Ralph Waldo Emerson visited New England Shaker villages, conversed with individual Shakers, and referred variously to the Shakers in lectures, letters, and journals. In a *Journal* entry of 1842, he coyly wrote: "At the Shaker's house in Harvard I found a spirit level on the windowseat a very good emblem for the society; but, unfortunately, neither the table, nor the shelf, nor the windowseat were plumb"[21] Emerson had a genius for figurative expression. For him, the spirit level left on the windowseat was a physical symbol that Shakerism fell short of its own expectations. Only so much can be made straight from the crooked timber of humanity. The Shakers recognized that the timber was crooked, but from it, anyway, sought to build a heaven on earth.

The religion behind the chair that Merton so much admired kept its eye on two worlds at once: the earthly and the heavenly. Its inspiration came from a woman who urged her followers to carry forward the work of building a heaven on earth that Jesus had begun. She was a savvy woman, who knew that what she urged was hard, and would take a long time to bring about. But her belief and optimism never waned. If you put your hands to work and your hearts to God, she proclaimed, "you will be helps to natural generations: yea, you may be helps to an hundred generations."[22]

When I reflect on the teachings of Ann Lee and the religion she inspired, I am reminded that a thousand-mile journey, regardless of its difficulty, begins with one forward step. So does the building of a heaven on earth.

NOTES

1. Thomas Merton, Introduction, *Religion in Wood: A book of Shaker Furniture*, Edward Deming Andrews and Faith Andrews (Bloomington and London: Indiana University Press, 1973), xiii.

2. Flo Morse, *The Shakers and the World's People* (Hanover and London: University Press of New England, 1980), 240.

3. Edward Robley Whitson, ed., *The Shakers: Two Centuries of Spiritual Reflection* (New York: Paulist Press, 1983), xi.

4. Frederick W. Evans, *Autobiography of a Shaker and Revelation of the Apocalypse*. With an Appendix. New and Enlarged Edition, with Portrait (Glasgow: United Publishing Co., 1888. Philadelphia: Porcupine Press, 1972), 8.

5. Evans, *Autobiography*, 20.

6. Evans, *Autobiography*, 23.

7. Henri Desroche, *The American Shakers: From Neo-Christianity to Presocialism*, trans. John K. Savacool (Amherst: The University of Massachusetts Press, 1971), 280.

8. Evans, *Autobiography*, 2.

9. Evans, *Autobiography*, v.

10. Evans, *Autobiography*, 26.

11. Evans, *Autobiography*, 48.

12. Evans, *Autobiography, 35.*

13. Evans, *Autobiography*, 36

14. Evans, *Autobiography*, 38.

15. Evans, *Autobiography*, 82.

16. Evans, *Autobiography*, 84.

17. Evans, *Autobiography*, 77.

18. Quoted in John McKelvie Whitworth, *God's Blueprints: A Sociological Study of Three Utopian Sects* (London: Routledge and Kegan Paul, 1975), 75.

19. Edward Deming Andrews, *The People Called Shakers* (New York: Oxford University Press, 1953), 224–40.

20. *Precepts of Mother Ann: Testimonies of the Life, Character, Revelations and Doctrines of MOTHER ANN LEE, and The ELDERS WITH HER, Through whom the word of Eternal life was opened in this day, of CHRIST'S SECOND APPEARING, Collected from Living Witnesses, in union with the Church,* 2ⁿᵈ ed. (Albany, N.Y.: Weed, Parsons & Co., Printers, 1888), 166.

21. Ralph Waldo Emerson. *The Journals and Miscellaneous Notebooks of Ralph Waldo Emerson,* Vol. VIII, 1841-1843, eds. William H. Gilman, J. E. Parsons (Cambridge, Massachusetts: Harvard University Press, 1970), 278-79.

22. *Precepts,* 214.

11

Ralph Waldo Emerson's Main Subject

The Bible will not be ended until the Creation is.

—Emerson, *The Journals and Miscellaneous Notebooks*, Volume XVI

R ALPH WALDO EMERSON was not wholly a scholar, wholly a philosopher, or wholly a poet, but a mixture of all three—a person of letters. Anyone who sets out to read all of Emerson faces a mountainous task. His work consists of multiple volumes containing sermons, lectures, poetry, essays, letters, notes, and journals.[1] As a college English major, dragooned into reading essays of Emerson, I found him hard to understand. Where were the filaments that linked one sentence to another? Why did the sentences contain such involved syntax? Why did Emerson repeatedly digress from the main subject? Indeed, what was the main subject? I offer here an overview of Emerson's life and literary accomplishment, with an expression in conclusion of what I hold dear as his main subject.

BEGINNINGS

Emerson, born in 1803, was the fourth of eight children, of whom three died in infancy. His father, William, was a Unitarian minister of the First Church in Boston. When Emerson was not quite eight, his father died. After the death of her husband, Ruth Haskins Emerson supported her five sons in genteel poverty by taking in boarders.

Mary Moody Emerson, Emerson's aunt, was a powerful ally to Ruth in the upbringing and education of the Emerson boys. Before he was three, Emerson attended Mrs. Whitwell's nursery school in Boston. Later he attended Lawson Lyon's grammar school. When he was nine, he entered Boston Latin School. A year later, because of the high cost of living in Boston, the family left the city to live in Concord. After a year in Concord, the family sent him back to Boston Latin School, where he spent the next two years preparing for college.

In 1817, Emerson entered Harvard College on a scholarship that provided room and board in return for his serving the President as a messenger and his waiting on tables at the Commons. Emerson was not a stellar student. In 1821, he graduated midway in a class of fifty-nine. As a source of income after leaving Harvard, he taught in private schools, first in Boston then in nearby villages. By 1827, after he had studied two years at Harvard Divinity School and had acquired a license to preach, he had put his days as a schoolteacher behind him.

Emerson was a conscientious schoolteacher, but clearly did not want school teaching as his vocation. "The duties," he said "were never congenial with my disposition."[2] He would eventually realize that neither were the duties of the ministry congenial with his disposition. In 1829, he became junior pastor of Boston's Second Church, and a short time later its senior pastor. But after three years at Second Church, depressed over the death of his young wife Ellen from tuberculosis, and in disagreement with his congregation over the celebration of the Lord's Supper, he resigned his pastorate and sailed for Europe in December 1832.

Months of travel took him to Italy, France, and England. Among the benefits of his travel were meetings with three literary figures he admired: Coleridge, Wordsworth, and Carlyle. In Carlyle he found a vibrant and mutual spirit, with whom he retained a life-long friendship.

During a visit to Paris in July of 1833, Emerson visited and marveled at the naturalist exhibitions at the Jardin des Plantes. When he returned to Concord in October of the same year, the Boston Society of Natural History invited him to present a public lecture. Drawing upon recollections of his visit to the Jardin des Plantes, and upon his own developing theory of a spiritual correspondence between man and nature, Emerson delivered at the Boston Masonic Temple in November of 1833 a lecture titled "The Uses of Natural History." With this public lecture Emerson found a professional activity that suited his disposition. Throughout the remainder of his life, his most dependable source of income was the lecture platform.[3]

THE LYCEUM

Emerson's primary forum for public lecturing was the Lyceum. Conceived as a form of adult education, the Lyceum movement emerged in 1826 in Millbury, Massachusetts, and numbered hundreds of local groups when Emerson started his lecturing career. The Lyceum movement coincided with a growing demand on the part of ordinary working people for a greater share in the material benefits of the expanding Republic. Emerson saw the ugly barren landscape of a commercial society rushing madly toward ever more senseless endeavor and consumption. It was against this social background that he evolved as a self-appointed teacher to the American public. He taught that people should temper their materialistic desires and strive to realize the deepest meanings and possibilities of human existence. Often he spoke over the heads of his audiences, but his manner was so alluring and the content of his lectures so uplifting that people were eager to hear him. Over the span of his career he presented before Lyceum and other audiences "nearly 1500 lectures in twenty-two states, Canada, England, and Scotland."[4]

In 1834, Emerson became a resident of Concord. For a year he lived with his mother in the gambrel-roofed house that overlooks the Concord River, built as a parsonage for his grandfather, who had served the Concord First Parish church. It was this house that Nathaniel Hawthorne later occupied and referred to in the title of his *Mosses from an Old Manse*. Emerson married Lydia Jackson of Plymouth in 1835, whom he called Lidian, and bought a house in Concord where they settled for life. Lidian Emerson had the patience of Penelope. Along with managing the household and tending the children, she tolerated all sorts of eccentric types who came to visit Emerson, often for extended periods of time.

TRANSCENDENTALISM

The New England culture from which Emerson sprang was rich in religious heritage. From the time of the arrival of the Puritans to near the end of the eighteenth century—roughly two centuries—the dominant mode of religious thought in America was Calvinistic. During the early years of the nineteenth century, however, Unitarianism, a non-Calvinistic mode of religious thought, spread over New England that rejected the traditional doctrines of the divinity of Christ and the Trinity. William Ellery Channing, a gifted Unitarian theologian, orator, and writer, articulated ideas about the sanctity of the individual conscience that influenced the Transcendentalists. These philosophical idealists regarded matter as an appearance and thought as the reality. They talked and wrote about truths that transcend ordinary human experience and ordinary knowledge; they advocated social, civil, and religious reform; and they advanced philanthropic causes.

In 1840, a group of Transcendentalists initiated the periodical, *The Dial*. Among its supporters and contributors were Margaret Fuller, Ralph Waldo Emerson, Amos Bronson Alcott—father of the novelist Louisa May Alcott—George Ripley, Theodore Parker, James Freeman Clarke, and Henry David Thoreau. The periodical ceased publication after four years for lack of financial support.

Margaret Fuller, editor of *The Dial* before Emerson succeeded her, was a dynamic figure among the Transcendentalists. She translated works from German, practiced journalism, lectured, and held her own with the ablest of thinkers, including Emerson. During a visit to Italy, she married in 1848 and bore a child to the Marquis Ossoli. In 1850, Fuller and her husband returned to America, but within sight of the American coast their ship wrecked in a storm, and the entire family drowned. In a brief life Fuller left her mark on American literature. Her work *Woman in the Nineteenth Century* reflects a social consciousness that anticipates feminist activism of the twentieth and twenty-first centuries.

WRITING HABITS

As a writer, Emerson was highly resourceful in the management of his materials. From his undergraduate days at Harvard, he made a practice of keeping carefully indexed journals and notebooks that recorded thoughts, images, sentences, and paragraphs. His essays are replete with pithy expressions drawn from journals and notebooks that serve as nodes of thought around which sentences congregate like pigeons coming home to roost. While Emerson borrowed from others, he constantly borrowed from himself, taking material from one place and putting it in another, nuancing the material to say differently what he had said previously.

NATURE

Emerson bought a forty-acre section of woods on Walden Pond—on the outskirts of Concord--as a place for solitary retreats, where he later gave Henry David Thoreau permission to build a cabin. Emerson as much as Thoreau was a lover of nature, but his approach to nature differed from Thoreau's. Thoreau in *Walden* is the keen observer *of* the natural world; Emerson in his essay "Nature" is the abstract thinker *about* the natural world.

Emerson published "Nature" anonymously in 1836, the first declaration of the Transcendentalist principles on which he based much of his writing. He writes:

The foregoing generations beheld God and nature face to face; we, through their eyes. Why should not we enjoy an original relation to the universe? Why should not we also enjoy an original relation to the universe? Why should not we have a poetry and philosophy of insight and not of tradition, and a religion by revelation to us, and not the history of theirs?[5]

These questions start the discussion in "Nature." Emerson goes on to speak of the varied ways humans are related to nature, under the headings of Commodity, Beauty, Language, Discipline, Spirit, and Prospects. Two crucial Transcendentalist principles that Emerson conveys in "Nature" are: (1) God is in all things; and, (2) God is present to human intuition and imagination.

PHI BETA KAPPA AND DIVINITY SCHOOL LECTURES

In 1837, Emerson delivered before the Phi Beta Kappa Society of Harvard College a lecture titled "The American Scholar." It was his challenge to academic ideals of that day, and a plea for the scholar to seek a personal vision of nature, to reject academic conventions inherited from the past, to have confidence in personal judgment, and to live a practical rather than a bookish life. Emerson read his lectures in a calm manner, evenly paced, with few gestures. Perhaps his manner of presenting this lecture so hypnotized his listeners that they failed to grasp its radical content. It undercut the very scholarly ideals for which the Phi Beta Kappa Society stood.

Even more radical in content was the "The Divinity School Address" that Emerson presented in 1838 to the graduating class of Harvard Divinity School. He told his audience of aspiring clergymen:

Historical Christianity has fallen into the error that corrupts all attempts to communicate religion. As it appears to us, and as it has appeared for ages, it is not the doctrine of the soul, but an exaggeration of the personal, the positive, the ritual. It has dwelt, it dwells, with noxious exaggeration about the *person* of Jesus.[6]

In this lecture Emerson essentially denied traditional understanding of the divinity of Jesus. Public outrage among religious conservatives was swift. It was thirty years before Harvard again invited him to speak within its precincts.

FIRST AND SECOND SERIES *ESSAYS* AND *REPRESENTATIVE MEN*

From manuscripts of his lectures Emerson derived the First and Second Series of his *Essays*. The First Series appeared in 1841. It included: "History," "Self-Reliance," Compensation," "Spiritual Laws," "Love," "Friendship," "Prudence," "Heroism," The Over-Soul," "Circles," "Intellect," and "Art." The Second Series, appeared in 1844. It included "The Poet," "Experience," "Character," "Manners," "Gifts," "Nature" (a second handling of this theme), "Politics," "Nominalist and Realist," and "The New England Reformers." The *Essays* of the First and Second Series persist as Emerson's most-read works.

In 1847, Emerson took a second trip to England and Scotland, this time to lecture to Lyceum audiences. The material of these lectures appeared in 1850 as *Representative Men*. As did Carlyle in his book *Heroes and Hero-Worship*, Emerson assumed that we learn general intellectual and moral truths about human nature from the study of famous persons. The persons he selected for study and interpretation in *Representative Men* were Plato, Swedenborg, Montaigne, Shakespeare, Napoleon, and Goethe.

English Traits and the Yin and Yang of Emerson's Thought

Emerson published *English Traits* in 1856, in which he produced a study of the English character. Emerson admired the English, but with reservations. *English Traits* has a "yes" and "no" quality about it that is often present in Emerson's writing. He seems to give with one hand while taking away with the other. Until the reader gets used to this characteristic, it can prove to be quite aggravating. It is possible to overcome this aggravation, however, once the reader sees that through his very style Emerson renders a vision of life similar to the Chinese vision of *yin* and *yang*. According to this vision, nothing in the universe is either all white or all black. Everything is a combination of two principles: male and female, good and evil, morality and immorality, knowledge and ignorance. He thought and wrote in terms of oppositions.

The Conduct of Life

The Conduct of Life, published in 1860, is diminished in the involved syntax of his early writing. *The Conduct of Life* contains three of his most philosophical essays, "Fate," "Power," and "Illusions." It is a book that had an influence on the German philosopher Friedrich Nietzsche for its emphasis on fate and power (will) as two perennial aspects of human existence.

Poetry

Emerson wrote poetry for years before publishing in 1846 his first collection, *Poems*. Some of my favorite poems in this collection are "The Problem," "Woodnotes I and II," "The Sphinx," "The Rhedora," and "Threnody." In 1867, he published a second collection, *May-Day and Other Poems.* In comparison with Whitman, Emerson is a poet of lower flights. But at his best, as in such poems as "Brahma," "My Garden," and "Boston Hymn" he holds a place among the most beloved of American poets.

EMERSON AND SLAVERY

Emerson's attitudes on slavery reveal a pattern of restraint in his personality. He spoke against slavery, but not aggressively against the South. He supported a plan to buy slaves from their legal owners as a practical step towards abolition. As a writer and public speaker, he tried to remain aloof of politics. He came to see, however, that if the Union were to survive, civil war was the looming outcome. With the passage of the Fugitive Slave Law of 1850—which enacted that runaway slaves were private property and had to be returned to their owners—Emerson's sense of individual freedom and self-culture, expressed in "Self Reliance," was cut to the quick. He became a leader in opposition to slavery, writing and speaking his antislavery convictions in many venues.[7]

FINAL WORKS

Harvard forgave Emerson for his "Divinity School Address," awarded him an honorary doctorate, and invited him to return to the college to deliver a series of lectures in 1868, 1869, and 1870. These lectures furnished the material for his book *Natural History of Intellect.* In 1870, he published *Society and Solitude.* Among the twelve essays included under this title is "Books," in which he advises, "Never read any [book] but what you like." It also includes the essay, "Civilization," which contains what is perhaps Emerson's most quoted line: "Hitch your wagon to a star!" In 1874, he published *Parnassus,* a collection of his favorite poems by British and American writers. And in 1875 he published, with the help of an editor, *Letters and Social Aims.*

EMERSON'S LAST YEARS

In 1871, Emerson visited California, where he met and conversed with the naturalist John Muir. Soon after his return to Concord, a fire partially destroyed the Emerson home, an event that shook him emotionally. During the lengthy process of the home's restoration, he took a last trip abroad, accompanied by his daughter Ellen, that included England and Egypt. At his homecoming in 1873, the entire town of Concord greeted him, and presented him with a gift of some twelve thousand dollars to help with the expense of the journey and restoration of the house.

In the last months of his life, he was unable to travel or to write much of anything. He stayed at home, entertained visitors, and took walks around Concord. He never descended into complete senility, and he maintained a positive attitude toward life. The end came on April 17, 1882, about a month short of his eightieth birthday on May 25. He had taken a walk on a chilly spring day that resulted in a cold, then pneumonia. At the time of his funeral, out of respect for Concord's most famous citizen, the people of the town draped their homes and the public buildings. His burial place in Concord's Sleepy Hollow Cemetery is on Authors' Ridge, a few steps away from the grave of Nathaniel Hawthorne and a short distance from the simple headstone marking the grave of Henry David Thoreau.

EMERSON'S MAIN SUBJECT

Emerson quit his pulpit for the writing desk and lecture platform, and consciously separated himself from the religion of his Puritan forefathers; but he retained in his own way that religion's call for "salvation," or for transformation from an "old" to a "new" way of life. In "The Divinity School Address," Emerson urged graduates of Harvard Divinity School not to settle in their ministerial professions for platitudes people might like to hear but that fail to awaken from customary religious slumber. Emerson revered the Bible as a sacred book, but was not bound by Christian doctrine in interpreting it. He commended a religion *of* Jesus rather than a religion *about* Jesus; and was clear in the address what he thought the religion of Jesus was:

> He saw with open eye the mystery of the soul. Drawn by its severe harmony, ravished with its beauty, he lived in it, and had his being there. . . . He saw that God incarnates himself in man. . . . He said, in this jubilee of sublime emotion, "I am divine. Through me, God acts; through me, speaks. Would you see God, see me; or see thee, when thou also thinkest as I now think."[8]

Jesus' religion, in Emerson's interpretation, was an opening of the eye of the mind to a sublimity that hovers over and seeps into every crevice of the creation. In the most famous—and often mocked—passage in "Nature," Emerson offers testimony to what salvation was for him:

> Standing on the bare ground—my head bathed by the blithe air, and uplifted into infinite space,—all mean egotism vanishes. I become a transparent eyeball. I am nothing. I see all. The currents of the Universal Being circulate through me; I am part or parcel of god. . . . I am the lover of uncontained and immortal beauty.[9]

The form of salvation Emerson describes is not release *from* Adamic guilt or sin, but release *unto* the mystery of a creation that is ever unfolding.

The airiness of Emerson's thought distances him from thinkers in contemporary culture for whom "what you see is what you get," a phrase that infers there is no *behindness* or *underneathness*, or *overness* to the world of appearances. It requires a certain letting-go to read Emerson: a willingness to give him space, to listen to him talk rather than interrupt him to talk back. One does not interrupt the preacher in the midst of the sermon. If there is a single sentence in Emerson that expresses the main subject of his thought, it is the one taped to the framed photograph of him that hangs on the wall above my desk: "We lie in the lap of immense intelligence, which makes us receivers of its truth and organs of its activity."[10]

NOTES

1. *The Collected Works of Ralph Waldo Emerson* is a scholarly project that was many years in the making. The *Collected Works* consists of numerous volumes, with numerous editors. The *Collected Works* are published by Harvard University, Belknap Press. I have drawn on these volumes, but for immediacy of accessibility, I draw on and cite Emerson's works from *Selections from Ralph Waldo Emerson: An Organic Anthology*, ed. Stephen E. Whicher, Boston: Houghton Mifflin Company Riverside Editions, 1960. This book is hereafter referenced with a title of Emerson's writing followed by *An Organic Anthology*.

2. James Elliot Cabot, *A Memoir of Ralph Waldo Emerson,* 2 vols. (Boston: Houghton, Mifflin and Company, 1887), Vol. 1, 75.

3. See Albert J. von Frank, *An Emerson Chronology*, 2 vols., 2nd edition (Albuquerque: Studio Non Troppo, 2016). In over 1100 pages, von Frank lays out the itinerary and activities of Emerson's life on virtually a daily basis from January 1, 1826 to April 27, 1882. Though he was a slight man, weighing around 155 pounds (*Chronology*, 724,) Emerson had considerable physical stamina. He had to have stamina to sustain his traveling and lecturing activities under traveling conditions that by present day standards were slow and toilsome. The *Chronology* indicates, for example (724–25), that in 1856, when he was fifty-three years old, he lectured on March 4 in Lincoln, Massachusetts; on March 5 in Cambridge, Massachusetts; on March 6 in Exeter, New Hampshire; on March 11 in Great Barrington, Massachusetts; on March 12 in Lee, Massachusetts; on March 13 in Pittsfield, Massachusetts; on March 14 in North Adams, Massachusetts; on March 20 in Hanover, New Hampshire; and on March 27 in Boston (*Chronology*, 724–25). The *Chronology* dispels any notion of Emerson as a man bound to a desk.

4. Merton M. Sealts, Jr., "Emerson as Teacher," *Ralph Waldo Emerson: A Collection of Critical Essays*. ed. Lawrence Buell (Englewood Cliffs, New Jersey: Prentice Hall, 1993), 203.

5. Emerson, "Nature," *An Organic Anthology*, 21.

6. Emerson, "The Divinity School Address," *An Organic Anthology*, 106.

7. These writings are conveniently available in a comprehensive and authoritative collection, *Ralph Waldo Emerson's Antislavery Writings*, eds. Len Gougeon and Joel Myerson (New Haven: Yale University Press, 2002).

8. Emerson, "Divinity School Address," *An Organic Anthology*, 105.

9. Emerson, "Nature," *An Organic Anthology*, 24.

10. Emerson, "Self-Reliance," *An Organic Anthology*, 156.

A TESTIMONIAL EPILOGUE

*There is in all visible things an invisible fecundity, a dimmed
light, a meek namelessness, a hidden wholeness. This mys-
terious Unity and Integrity is Wisdom, the Mother of all,
Natura naturans.*

—Thomas Merton, "Hagia Sophia"

I grew up among evangelical Protestants who read the Bible as the
Word of God speaking to them through its pages. The Bible study
group of our church met regularly in my parents' home. The participants arrived in the evening with their King James Bibles in hand.
Against a wall they leaned a large chart that guided them in their
reading of biblical passages. Individual members within the group
offered testimony to how a particular passage spoke to him or her.
I was too young to participate in the conversation, but to this day I
value the group's example of listening to the Bible, as one might listen
to any sacred text, as speaking to oneself.

Passages within the Bible that speak to me tell the story of creation. By the phrase "story of creation" I refer to a narrative initiated
in Genesis 1–3 that threads through the Bible in various formula-
tions in such passages as Psalm 8; Proverbs 8; Job 40–41; Isaiah 40:
21–22; Matthew 6: 25–34, Romans 8: 18–25, and Revelation 22: 1–5.
The "tree of life" (Gen. 2:9) planted in the Garden of Eden is the
same "tree of life" (Rev. 22: 2) replanted in the Heavenly City of the
New Jerusalem in Revelation.

The story of the creation the Bible tells is nowhere recorded in
nature; nature has no story except the story humans attribute to it.
The biblical writers were not present *in the beginning.* Out of inspiration
and imagination they told of a world of nature that is "appointed,"

or ordained; is inherent with energies essential to all life; is of limited duration, having a beginning, middle, and end; and is revelatory of divine Wisdom.

There is a *back then* character to the biblical story of creation, but the creation did not end back then. The Wisdom that was active in the beginning is still active in the here and now. Wisdom is elusive; it reveals itself in multiple guises. The writers I consider in this book are alert to Wisdom, though they reference it by other than its biblical name. Jefferies speaks of *something more subtle than electricity*; Roethke of the *urge* within all life; Jeffers of the *wild God*; Wilson of *the grace rooted solidly on Earth*; Hubbard of the *One who made the river*; Berry of the *divine economy*; Bromfield of *the things that count*; Shakespeare of the *music of the spheres*; Thomas of the *hidden God;* Mother Ann Lee of the *Gospel in the heart*; and Emerson of the *immense intelligence*.

We live in the "Environmental Age." The celebration of the first Earth Day in 1970 signaled wide public recognition of our human separation from the whole of nature. The genre of environmental writing over the past half century is filled with facts and laments about this separation, and with urgings to reconnect to the whole of nature in our thoughts and behaviors. The environmentalist slogan of our time to *save the earth* is impossibly ambitious. We cannot save the earth; it has its own cosmological destiny. But we can look to the biblical story of creation for its power to move us to reflection on a world of nature we inherit rather than make, and on *something* within nature to which we owe observance and gratitude for the on-going of life.

I owe to my former teacher Joseph Sittler the following insight:

To use a thing is to make it instrumental to a purpose, and some things are to be so used. To enjoy a thing is to permit it to be what it is prior to and apart from any instrumental assessment of it, and some things are to be so enjoyed.[1]

Enjoyment of things of the earth is aligned with the biblical imperatives both to *subdue,* or use, and to *keep* them. Of necessity we must
make instrumental use of things for our material needs. But when
our instrumental use of things is excessive, we neglect what it means
to keep them. To keep things is to enjoy them in heart and mind for
what they are in themselves beyond human use, and to let them *be.*
Professor Sittler never tired of referring to Gerard Manley Hopkins
for the poet's ability to penetrate the obviousness of things to *something* that made each thing wondrous to contemplate as a unique
contributor to the fulsomeness of nature. In his poem "The Starlit
Night," Hopkins writes:

> Look at the stars! Look, look up at the skies!
> O look at all the fire-folk sitting in the air!
> The bright boroughs, the circle–citadels there!
> Down in dim woods the diamond delves! The elve's–eyes!
> The grey lawns cold where gold, where quickgold lies!
> Wind–beat whitebeam! Airy abeles set on a flare!
> Flake-doves sent floating forth at a farmyard scare!—
> Ah well! It is all a purchase, all is a prize.[2]

We inhabit a lagniappe earth, where "lives the dearest freshness deep
down things."[3] That message is as old as the biblical story of creation,
and as fresh as the Wisdom of the earth that is new every morning.

Notes

1. Joseph Sittler, *Evocations of Grace: Writings on Ecology, Theology and Ethics,* eds. Steven Bouma–Prediger and Peter Bakken (Grand Rapids, Michigan: William B. Eerdmans Publishing Company, 2000), 56.
2. Gerard Manley Hopkins, "The Starlight Night." *The Poems of Gerard Manley Hopkins,* eds. W. H. Gardner and N. H. Mackenzie. 4th ed. (London: Oxford University Press, 1967), 66.
3. Hopkins, "God's Grandeur," *The Poems of Gerard Manley Hopkins,* 66.

BIBLIOGRAPHY

Andrews, Edward Deming. *The People Called Shakers*. New York: Oxford University Press, 1953.

Baillie, Donald. *Our Knowledge of God*. New York: Charles Scribner's Sons, 1959.

Bate, Jonathan. *The Song of the Earth*. Cambridge, Massachusetts: Harvard University Press, 2000.

Bede. *Ecclesiastical History of the English People*. Translated by *Leo Sherley-Price* and revised by R. E. Latham. New York: Penguin Books, 1990.

Berry, Wendell. "The Agrarian Standard." In *Citizenship Papers*. Washington DC: Shoemaker and Hoard, 2003.

———. *Another Turn of the Crank: Essays by Wendell Berry*. Washington, D. C.: Counterpoint, 1995.

———. "Christianity and the Survival of Creation." In *Sex, Economy, and Community* New York: Pantheon Books, 1993.

———. "The Gift of Good Land." In *The Gift of Good Land*. New York: North Point Press, Farrar, Straus and Giroux, 1981.

———. *Harlan Hubbard: Life and Work*. New York: Pantheon Books, 1990.

———. *Jayber Crow*. Washington D.C.: Counterpoint, 2000.

——. *The Memory of Old Jack*. Washington, D.C.: Counterpoint, 1999.

——. *Remembering*. San Francisco: North Point Press, 1988.

——. *A Timbered Choir: The Sabbath Poems* 1979-1997. Washington D.C.: Counterpoint, 1998.

——. *The Unsettling of America: Culture and Agriculture*. San Francisco: Sierra Club Books, 1986.

Bromfield, Louis. *Animals and Other People*. New York: Harper and Brothers, 1955.

——. *The Farm*. N.Y: Aeonian Press, 1976.

——. *From My Experience*. Wooster, Ohio: The Wooster Book Company, 1999.

——. *Pleasant Valley*. Wooster, Ohio: The Wooster Book Company, 1997.

——. "Up Ferguson Way." In *The World We Live In: Stories by Louis Bromfield*. Philadelphia: The Blakiston Company, 1944.

Buell, Lawrence. *The Environmental Imagination: Thoreau, Nature Writing, and the Formation of American Culture*. Cambridge, Massachusetts: The Belknap Press of Harvard University Press, 1996.

Cabot, James Elliot. *A Memoir of Ralph Waldo Emerson*. Vol. 1. Boston: Houghton, Mifflin and Company, 1887.

Carson, Rachel. *Silent Spring.* Boston: Houghton Mifflin Company, 1962.

Cather, Willa. *My Antonia.* Boston: Houghton Mifflin Company, 1954.

Caudill, Harry M. *Night Comes to the Cumberlands.* Boston: Little, Brown and Co., 1963.

De Quincey, Thomas. *Leaders in Literature with Notice of Traditional Errors Affecting Them.* Edinburgh: Adam and Charles Black, 1887.

Desroche, Henri. *The American Shakers: From Neo-Christianity to Presocialism.* Translated by John K. Savacool. Amherst: The University of Massachusetts Press, 1971.

Dyer, T. F. Thiselton. *Folk-Lore of Shakespeare.* New York: Dover Publications, Inc., 1966.

Eiseley, Loren. "Foreword." In *Not Man Apart: Photographs of the Big Sur Coast, With Lines from Robinson Jeffers.* Edited by David Bower. San Francisco: Sierra Club, 1965.

Eliade, Mircea. *Myths, Dreams, and Mysteries: The Encounter Between Contemporary Faiths and Archaic Realities.* New York: Harper Torchbooks, Harper and Row, 1960.

Eliot, T. S. [Thomas Stearns]. *Complete Poems and Plays: 1909-1950.* New York: Harcourt, Brace and Company, 1952.

Ellacombe, Henry Nicholson. *The Plant-Lore and Garden-Craft of Shakespeare.* London: W. Satchell and Co., 1884.

Emerson, Ralph Waldo. *The Journals and Miscellaneous Notebooks of Ralph Waldo Emerson.* Edited by Gilman, William H. and J. E. Parsons. Vol. VIII. Cambridge, Massachusetts: The Belknap Press of Harvard University Press, 1970.

——. *The Journals and Miscellaneous Notebooks of Ralph Waldo Emerson.* Edited by Bosco, Ronald A. and Glen M. Johnson, Vol. XVI. Cambridge Massachusetts: The Belknap Press of Harvard University Press, 1982.

——. *Ralph Waldo Emerson's Antislavery Writings.* Edited by Gougeon, Len and Joel Myerson. New Haven: Yale University Press, 2002.

——. *Selections from Ralph Waldo Emerson: An Organic Anthology.* Edited by Stephen E. Whicher. Boston: Houghton Mifflin Company, Riverside Editions, 1960.

Felstiner, John. *Can Poetry Save the Earth? A Field Guide to Nature Poems.* New Haven and London: Yale University Press, 2009.

Fuller, Margaret. *Women in the Nineteenth Century.* Edited by Joslyn T. Pine. New York: Dover Thrift Editions, 1999.

Geld, Ellen Bromfield. *The Heritage: A Daughter's Memories of Louis Bromfield.* Athens, Ohio: Ohio University Press, 1999.

Hardy, Thomas. *Tess of the d'Urbervilles.* Edited by Scott Elledge. New York: W. W. Norton and Company, 1965.

——. *Far From the Madding Crowd*. Introduction by Roesemarie Morgan. New York: Penguin Books, 2000.

Hubbard, Harlan. *Journals 1929-1944*. Edited by Kohler, Vincent and David F. Ward. Lexington, Kentucky: The University of Kentucky Press, 1987.

——. *Payne Hollow: Life on the Fringe of Society*. Frankfort, Kentucky: Gnomen Press, 1974.

——. *Payne Hollow Journal*. Edited by Don Wallis, with illustrations by the author. Lexington, Kentucky: The University Press of Kentucky, 1996.

——. *Shantyboat: A River Way of Life*. Lexington, Kentucky: The University of Kentucky Press, 1953.

——. *Shantyboat on the Bayous*. With illustrations by the author and a Foreword by Don Wallis. Lexington, Kentucky: The University Press of Kentucky, 1990.

——. *The Woodcuts of Harlan Hubbard*. From the Collection of Bill Caddell with a Foreword by Wendell Berry. Lexington, Kentucky: The University Press of Kentucky, 1994.

Jackson, Wes. *Nature as Measure: The Selected Essays of Wes Jackson*. Introduction by Wendell Berry. Berkeley, CA: Counterpoint, 2011.

Jefferies, Richard. *Bevis: The Story of a Boy*. Introduction by Henry Williamson. London: J. M. Dent and Sons LTD., 1981.

———. "The Country Sunday." In *Field and Hedgerow: Being the Last Essays*. London: Longman, Green, and Co., 1892.

——. *The Story of My Heart*. Edited by Samuel J. Looker. London: Constable Publishers, 1947.

——. "Walks in the Wheat-Fields." In *Field and Hedgerow: Being The Last Essays*. London: Longmans, Green, and Co., 1892.

——. "Wild Flowers." In *The Open Air*. London: Lutterworth Press, 1948.

Jeffers, Robinson. *The Selected Poetry of Robinson Jeffers*. Edited by Tim Hunt. Stanford University Press, 2001.

Jefferson, Thomas. *Notes on the State of Virginia*. New York: Penguin Putnam Books, 1999.

Keith W. J. *Richard Jefferies: A Critical Study*. Toronto: University of Toronto Press, 1965.

Kline, David. *Great Possessions: An Amish Farmer's Journal*. Foreword by Wendell Berry. New York: North Point Press, 1990.

Lewis, R. W. B. *The American Adam: Innocence, Tragedy, and Tradition in the Nineteenth Century*. Chicago: The University of Chicago Press, 1959.

Logsdon, Gene. *The Man Who Created Paradise: A Fable*. Foreword by Wendell Berry. Athens, Ohio: Ohio University Press, 1998.

——. Introduction. In Louis Bromfield's *Pleasant Valley*. Wooster, Ohio: The Wooster Book Company, 1997.

Merton, Thomas. Introduction. In *Religion in Wood: A book of Shaker Furniture*. Edited by Andrews, Edward Deming and Faith Andrews. Bloomington: Indiana University Press, 1973.

Milton, John. *The Riverside Milton*. Edited by Roy Flannigan. Boston: Houghton Mifflin Company, 1998.

Morse, Flo. *The Shakers and the World's People*. Hanover: University Press of New England, 1980.

Naess, Arne. *Ecology, Community and Lifestyle: Outline of an Ecosophy*. Translated and edited by David Rothenberg. New York: Cambridge University Press, 1995.

Phillips, D. Z. [Dewi Zephaniah]. *R. S. Thomas: Poet of the Hidden God*. London: The Macmillan Press Ltd., 1986.

Precepts of Mother Ann: Testimonies of the Life, Character, Revelations and Doctrines of MOTHER ANN LEE, and The ELDERS WITH HER, Through whom the word of Eternal life was opened in this day, of CHRIST'S SECOND APPEARING, Collected from Living Witnesses, in union with the Church. Second Edition. Albany, N.Y.: Weed, Parsons and Co., 1888.

Rees, Martin. *Our Cosmic Habitat*. Princeton: Princeton University Press, 2001.

Roethke, Theodore. *The Collected Poems of Theodore Roethke*. New York: Anchor Doubleday, 1975.

——. *The Lost Son and other poems by Theodore Roethke*. London: John Lehman Ltd., 1949.

——. *On the Poet and his Craft*. Edited by Ralph J. Mills, Jr. Seattle, Washington: The University of Washington Press, 1975.

——. *Selected Letters of Theodore Roethke*. Edited by Ralph J. Mills, Jr. Seattle, Washington: The University of Washington Press, 1968.

——. *Straw for the Fire: From the Notebooks, 1943-63*. Edited by David Wagoner. New York: Doubleday and Company, Inc., 1972.

Rogers, Byron. *The Man Who Went Into the West: The Life of R. S. Thomas*. London: Arum Press Limited, 2007.

Sanders, Scott Russell. *Staying Put: Making a Home in a Restless World*. Boston: Beacon Press, 1993.

The Shakers: Two Centuries of Spiritual Reflection. Edited by Edward Robley Whitson. New York: Paulist Press, 1983.

Schweitzer, Albert. *Out of My Life and Thought*. Translated by Antje Bultmann Lemke. Baltimore: The Johns Hopkins University Press, 2009.

Sealts, Merton M. Jr. "Emerson as Teacher." In *Ralph Waldo Emerson: A Collection of Critical Essays*. Edited by Lawrence Buell. Englewood Cliffs, New Jersey: Prentice Hall, 1993.

Shakespeare, William. *The Riverside Shakespeare*. Edited by G. Blakemore Evans. Boston: Houghton Mifflin Company, 1974.

Sittler, Joseph. *Evocations of Grace: Writings on Ecology, Theology and Ethics.* Edited by Bouma–Prediger, Steven and Peter Bakken. Grand Rapids, Michigan: William B. Eerdmans Publishing Company, 2000.

Stein, Stephen J. *The Shaker Experience in America: A History of the United Society of Believers.* New Haven: Yale Universtiy, Press, 1992.

St. John De Crèvecoeur, J. Hector. *Letters from an American Farmer and Sketches of Eighteenth Century America.* New York: Viking Penguin Inc., 1981.

Taylor, Charles. *A Secular Age.* Cambridge, Massachusetts: Belknap-Harvard University Press, 2007.

Thomas, R. S. [Ronald Stuart]. *Collected Poems: 1945–1990.* London: Phoenix Orion House, 1993.

——. *Collected Later Poems: 1988–2000.* Northumberland: Bloodaxe Books Ltd., 2013.

——. "R. S. Thomas: Autobiographical Essay." In *Miraculous Simplicity.* Edited by William V. Davis. Fayetteville: The University of Arkansas Press, 1993.

——. "R. S. Thomas: Priest and Poet." Transcript of John Ormand's film for BBC television, broadcast 2 April 1972. *Poetry Wales* (Spring 1972).

———. *R. S. Thomas: Selected Prose.* Edited by Sandra Anstey. Bridgend: Poetry of Wales Press, 1986.

———. "A Year in LLŷn." In *Autobiographies.* Translated by Jason Walford Davies from the Welsh. London: J. M. Dent, 1997.

Thoreau, Henry David. *Henry David Thoreau: Letters to a Spiritual Seeker.* Edited by Bradley P. Dean. New York: W. W. Norton and Company, 2004.

———. *Walden.* New York: The Heritage Press, 1939.

Tolstoy, Leo. "How Much Land Does a Man Need?" In *The Kreutzer Sonata and Other Short Stories.* New York: Dover Publications, 1993.

———. *Tolstoy on Shakespeare: A Critical Essay on Shakespeare* Translated by Tchertkoff, V. and I. F. M. Gloucester. United Kingdom: Dodo Press, n.d.

Von Frank, Albert J. *An Emerson Chronology.* Second Edition, 2 vols. Albuquerque: Studio Non Troppo, 2016.

Whitman, Walt. *Specimen Days and Collect.* New York: Dover Publications, Inc., 1995.

Whitworth, McKelvie. *God's Blueprints: A Sociological Study of Three Utopian Sects.* London: Routledge and Kegan Paul, 1975.

Wilson, E. O. [Edward Osborne]. *The Creation: An Appeal to Save Life on Earth*. New York: W. W. Norton and Company, 2006.

——. *Naturalist*. Washington, D. C.: Island Press, 1994.

Wood, Michael. *In Search of Shakespeare*. London: BBC Books, 2005.

ENOUGH

Looking up at leaves,
I find that I am satisfied
with simple green,
godly in its keeping me secure
belly up on the weathered swing.

So much can be said
of Holsteins leaning into hills.
The black and white
of things
make no mistake
of who you are,
where you're going,
where you're not.
The trail back to the barn
is brief.

And what about the lazy rye
sleeping under certain sun?
Tomorrow it will be there,
and I will walk slowly
to fetch the scythe.

—Freda M. Chaney

Made in the USA
Monee, IL
03 September 2021